Playing Leapfrog with Porcupines

By

Maynard Good Stoddard

© 2002 by Maynard Good Stoddard. All rights reserved.

No part of this book may be reproduced, stored in a retrieval system, or transmitted by any means, electronic, mechanical, photocopying, recording, or otherwise, without written permission from the author.

ISBN: 0-7596-9103-7

This book is printed on acid free paper.

1stBooks - rev. 3/18/02

ACKNOWLEDGMENT

I am not entirely at fault for the preparation of this fourth book in the series of Maynard Good Stoddard's shortcomings and the reasons for them.

Joe and Jayne Morales have bent over backwards (no easy trick in Joe's case) to get it into production. This being Joe's only exercise for some time, he should be thanking me. But you know how shortsighted some people are.

Fortunately, his dear wife more than atones for his many faults. Put them all together, therefore, they spell a wonderful couple. And this book wouldn't have been possible without their help.

Thus if you don't care for it, you'll know who to blame. (Or should it be "whom". I'll have to ask Jayne.)

Chapter 1

HAND-ME-DOWN GENES

Whenever convenient, we stay at motels offering a "free" breakfast, trying not to think that the cost lies buried in the bowels of the bill. But that's neither here nor there.

Where is it then, you ask? Just keep your shirt on, we'll get to it.

The problem is, the freeloader is required to draw his own orange juice, collect his own cereal, toast his own bagel, and stuff like that. The second problem is, I'm no good at stuff like that. And I'll be the first to point it out. (Make that the second to point it out. No need to tell you who is first.)

The fault lies not entirely with me. When genes for operating things of a mechanical nature were handed out, my early ancestors must have been out back, possibly inventing a square wheel to be used when they weren't going anywhere. Actually, I need to go back no further than the previous generation.

"She's not hitting on all four," my father announced one day, referring to our Model T Ford Touring Car. His knowing that the car had four cylinders was a triumph in itself. But over Mother's advice against it, he removed the spark plugs, then with one of her paring knives scraped off the carbon deposits. In so doing, to his amazement, he discovered that the points on the plugs did not meet.

"No wonder," he remarked, reaching for the pliers. Mechanics, of course, are trained to space the points to the nth degree. Dad, on the other hand, chose to squeeze the points tightly together. And then, with a great sigh of satisfaction, exclaimed, "There!"

When "she" then refused to hit on so much as one, never mind four, he decided he must have put the plugs back in the wrong holes. After numbering the holes and the plugs, he spent the morning attempting to return each plug to its "home" hole.

Not until Mother called in Bill Williams, our local garage man, were the plugs properly spaced and our "tin lizzie" hitting on all four again.

Dad had no better luck with our first radio, a Capehart, as I recall. I don't recall the call letters of the station we tuned in most frequently at that time (KDKA comes to mind), but I do remember that the squawks and squeals came all the way from Pittsburgh to our aerial in little old Richfield Center, Michigan.

When the static didn't come in clearly enough to suit him, Dad had this ritual of first stomping on the floor. If that didn't improve the reception, he would begin slapping the set until Mother made him stop. The Capehart soon developed a complex, refusing to cease squawking and squealing after being turned off.

Putting his head together, Dad decided that the noises had been left over in the aerial. To his nightly chores of shoving the dog out and checking to see if the house was on fire, thus was added the duty of disengaging the aerial. "To let it drain," he explained.

Mother, by this time, had given up calling upon Dad for assistance in matters that involved things of a mechanical nature. For instance, when our dog, Belle, got her tail caught in the cogs of the washing machine.

Walking past the machine on this washday morning and wagging her bushy tail in greeting to Mother, her long hairs got caught in the cogs and wound her tail about halfway up to her rump. Leaving dear old Dad to restrain the dog from pulling her tail off altogether, Mother ran next door, where Frank Cross, our friendly blacksmith, was shoeing a horse. She screamed, "Our dog is in the washing machine!"

Laying a hot horseshoe back on the anvil, removing his pipe from his mouth and spitting expertly into a keg of sawdust, Frank casually remarked, "That's a h—of a place for a dog."

Though Dad carefully watched the blacksmith's every move as he turned the cogs backward and set the dog free, it was knowledge down the drain. Even after the bald section of her tail

Playing Leapfrog with Porcupines

had recovered its hair, Belle never again went past the machine, idle or running, without giving it as wide a detour as possible.

Well, like father like son, as the saying goes. Which returns us to the free breakfast at motels.

I refer in particular to a free breakfast I underwent not too long ago at the Comfort Inn in Richmond, Indiana. Not that I am complaining about any shortage of comfort as far as the inn is concerned, let me hastily add. I blame only my shortage of genes in the do-it-yourself department.

After watching fellow breakfasters press down on the handle of an orange juice dispenser and seeing orange juice dispensed into their paper cups, I finally found the nerve to walk boldly up, position my cup, and cockily press down on the handle. It came off in my hand. After working unsuccessfully to restore it, I had no alternative but to stick it behind the dispenser. Although I got no orange juice, at least I had the satisfaction of knowing that no one else got orange juice from that time forward.

For my next act, I inserted two halves of a bagel into the toaster oven. The word 'TOAST" already aligned on the operational doohickey, I stood there and waited for the bagel to toast. And I stood there. And stood there. And people stood there and stood there behind me, waving their bagels and waffles whenever I looked around. I might be standing there yet, as a matter of fact, had not my dear wife laid down her sweet roll and come over to pull down the handle that put the toaster in business.

Later, now wise to the ways of the dumb thing and the crowd having thinned, I brought a second bagel to the toaster, stuck it in, smugly pulled down the 'TOAST" handle, and waited. And waited. Methodically, dear wife finally downed her sugared doughnut, worked her way through my accumulated audience, turned a knob from "OFF" to "400," and the bagel began toasting.

I am now sitting at my desk, having spent the past half hour trying to tape the bulb part of the floor lamp to the standard from which it has fallen. Walking past the open doorway to my dungeon and noticing the ribbons of tape streaming from my elbows, my dear wife stepped in and put the bulb part back on the standard simply by screwing it in. As she patiently pointed out, by being continually swiveled from my desk to the typewriter, the bulb section had become unscrewed.

If my dexterity-impaired genes went back no further than my father, there might be hope that one day I might still successfully step up and toast a bagel all by myself. But then I think of my grandfather, Fred, and the time he tried to progress from horse flesh to horse power by means of our Model T Ford Touring Car.

The "tin lizzie," as it was called—among other things—had been parked that day in the shade of a maple tree bordering our driveway. His driver ed limited entirely to observation, Grandfather's genes nevertheless must have assured him that he could drive the car up the ramp and through the double doors of the barn where the car was housed (or barned, in deference to you English students).

To our amazement, he not only got the engine started, but elected the proper pedal among the clutch, reverse, and brake on the floorboards at the driver's feet. Then hit the open doors of the barn dead center.

It was only after the T had disappeared into the dusty interior that his desperate yell came echoing off the stacks of baled hay: "WHOA!...WHOA!...WHOA!...I SAY."

Fortunately, a stack of loose hay at the back of the barn held the damage to no more than a leaky radiator and headlamps now ideally adjusted for hunting coon.

I have no way of knowing, of course, in what era our family's genes for dealing with things of a mechanical nature went off the track. For the untidy sum of $20, I once had our lineage traced back to William the Conqueror.

If it is true that he was one of us, how he managed to conquer remains a mystery. I suspect there must have been a Mrs. William the Conqueror. And it was she who showed him how to fit an arrow to the bow. And after he had stood there and waited...and waited...she finally put down her tea cake and patiently explained how to send it off.

Chapter 2

GRIME AND PUNISHMENT

Before we begin, I want to say something. I have no argument with the adage "cleanliness is next to godliness." I merely want to point out that in my early days (how early is none of your business), cleanliness was next to impossible. I'm pointing this out so that you of today with your big fat Jacuzzis, your pink heart-shaped bathtubs, your hot and cold running water, and your $20 bar of Gucci soap will count your blessings. You never will have to experience the Saturday-night ritual of trying to shed the week's accumulation of grime in a galvanized washtub using a slab of homemade soap that for both quantity and quality made you long for the lather of a hot horse.

Now that I've said that, we can get down to the nitty-gritty (accent on gritty).

Yes, the bathtub had been invented before I was. I'm not *that* old, for pete's sake! But the truth is (which may sound strange, coming from me), the early bathtub had three strikes against it, right off the bat. The prudes infesting those dark ages claimed the appliance to be immoral. Doctors labeled it unsanitary. The common council in one city went so far as to vote on a proposition that would prohibit bathing altogether from November 1 to March 15. For still other reasons why a store-bought bathtub never graced the Stoddard kitchen, I take you now to my copy of the Sears, Roebuck and Co. catalogue dated 1908, page 653. (Maybe my dear wife is right—I'd better get rid of some of this junk before I trip over it and break a leg.)

We can rule out price right away, as your basic steel tub with enamel coating could have graced our kitchen for a reasonable $6.75. For families that wanted to show off, there was the $28 job— "a Roll Rim White Enamel Tub, complete with No. 4 ½ Fuller Combination Cock." (Don't ask, because I don't know.)

Playing Leapfrog with Porcupines

Moving right along, next came the combined shower and tub, "the shower rising majestically at one end, the tub extending out some four feet." The copy neglects to add that the tub could be distinguished from the Eskimo kayak by a cover that fit over the entrance hole. Nor was there a warning that in case of unexpected company the bather ran the risk of sequestering himself in that thing until he wrinkled to death. Unless he chose to "rise up majestically" and take his chances.

Even less of a temptation would have been the tub that folded up against the wall during the week, to be lowered by ropes and pulleys for the bathing ceremonies on Saturday night. The problem here, as I may have already pointed out, is that the genes in our family didn't run to operating ropes and pulleys. The genes in our family ran more to storing stuff on any convenient elevated surface. By the time Saturday night rolled around, one look at the week's accumulation and forget it!

As for the "sofa-bath," forget that, too. A sofa through-out the week, on Saturday nights—presto chango—it converted into a bathing facility. Not at our house, buddy. I can see dear old Dad standing there with the "Sofa-Bath Manual" and saying to dear old Mom, "Can you make head or tail of this confounded thing?" The thought also might have crossed their respective minds—horror of horrors—of providing the visiting preacher and his wife a midweek baptism in the unholy water from the preceding Saturday night.

The point is...what *is* the point? I know it's around here somewhere. Oh, yes. Should you by now have got the idea that we did our body laundering down at the creek, it really wasn't that bad. In many ways it was worse.

Our weekly rendezvous with soap—as Mother chose to call it—and water began with a search for the battered old galvanized tub. Checking its rightful place, hanging from a spike on the back porch, would be a waste of time. Could it be just over the back fence, where it served to water the cows? No? Then how about under the maple tree, swimming with feathers from the chickens that had been scalded and plucked for Sunday dinner?

Still no luck? Perhaps in the garden, loaded with cucumbers, waiting to be lugged up to the house. Or in the cellar, where a bunch of bullheads were still doing nicely a day out of Flint River. Or in the shed, where we were conducting a scientific experiment to see if horse hairs left in water turned into snakes.

Although the years were not kind to the tub, yet another experiment by my two older brothers was responsible for reducing the tub's capacity the most number of gallons. I didn't get in on the project, primarily because I doubted if a cat in a washtub suspended from four balloons could actually make it from the peak of our barn roof into outer space. Fortunately, the cat had the smarts to bail out before its number of lives lessened by one ninth. Although the tub suffered its worst beating, like the abused Model T Ford in *Tobacco Road*, "it didn't hurt the runnin' of it none."

Eventually located and relieved of its cucumbers, feathers, bullheads, horse hairs or contents du jour, the tub would be filled by the head of the household lowering a bucket into the cistern and pulling up—oh, sometimes as much as 90 percent water. The stuff having arrived at the cistern via gutter and downspout, the remaining 10 percent was made up mainly of leaves and twigs, always a belly-up spider or two, an occasional frog, not infrequently a clumsy chipmunk, and on one memorable Saturday, the bucket came up adorned with a three-foot green snake.

Following clarification of this brew, dear old Dad would ceremoniously bear the tub into the kitchen and hoist it atop the range, griddles already hotter than that place mentioned in the Bible. While the—let's call it water—heated, the table would be pushed back against the cupboard wall, and the floor covered up to three pages deep with the *Flint Daily Journal* and the *Davison Index*, with the *Breeder's Gazette* filling in spaces where linoleum still stared up at us. This strategy, designed to prevent a possible overflow from the tub running downhill into the dining room, would go downhill itself whenever the sire of our little group would misjudge the heat index of the handles when

Playing Leapfrog with Porcupines

lifting the tub from the stove (too hot to handle, as it's known in baseball circles). We considered it lucky if the surf at high tide stopped short of the living room and the parental bedroom doors.

Anyway, back to the cistern...

There being four of us kids to come clean, or reasonably so, the first one to be secluded in the kitchen with the enduring tub of water stood the best chance of doing so. My sister being a girl, as sisters often were in those days, she always led the parade. We three boys followed, oldest to youngest. You guessed it: I came at the tail end.

Boys of today enjoy their very own batch of water, warm and sudsy, with little rubber duckies for companions and little plastic boats to sail across the surface. Not only did the temperature of the stuff I inherited on those memorable Saturday nights fall somewhat short of lukewarm, but if I'd had a windup toy soldier, it could have walked across without so much as getting its feet wet.

Upon my emergence from the kitchen—in record-setting time, I needn't point out—the tub was carried to the peony bed and the muck dumped out—if it would come out. Whether the stuff ever made it to the roots is doubtful. But surely no flower bed was ever blessed with richer topsoil.

At the time, I thought that my dad's dad, who lived with us in his latter days, had the most sensible idea when it came to this weekly threat of soap and water. "A change of socks is as good as a bath, any old time," he would announce to one and all, but especially to Mother, who kept complaining to Dad that "your father turns far paler at the sight of bathwater than he ever does from its effects."

Only once, on a Sunday morning after Gramps had evidently turned his palest at the sight of bathwater, did dear Old Dad rise to the occasion. Reheating the tub of water, he planned to carry it into the bedroom before the old gentleman could change his socks and call it a week. Dad might have made it, too, in spite of the increasing heat of the handles quickening his pace at every step, had he not tripped over Belle, our German shepherd, lying in her favorite spot beside the coal stove in the living room. The end result saw the head of the household go charging through the open bedroom door and slucing his father, hurrying to change his socks, across the bed and up against the wall. But "it didn't hurt the runnin' of him none."

By way of apology, Gramps was cleared for a change of socks on a regular schedule, without hassle. If the schedule also called for another bath, it was not posted on the refrigerator door. And yet the old fellow lived to the ripe—and I do mean ripe—age of 96. All things considered, who then can argue that his sock-changing theory was all wet?

Not I.

Chapter 3

FLEAS ARE NO CIRCUS

I don't claim to be an authority on cat behavior. I claim only that when a cat spends half its time scratching and biting and tying itself into a knot doing so, the cat must be trying to tell us something.

My reason for such speculation I credit to the two cats we are currently supporting. "Cracker," left by our daughter Shari when she moved to a "no pets allowed" townhouse in South Carolina, is a sexually impaired male; "White Cat," a sojourner who dropped in on us at least ten years ago, had evidently been spayed. (Not that these intimacies are relevant. Except to the cats, of course.)

What *is* relevant to this somber essay has been described by Noah Webster as "any of various small, wingless, bloodsucking insects of the order of Siphonaptera that have legs adapted for jumping and are parasitic on warm-blooded animals." It is these bloodsucking siphonapteras and their parasitics that are causing our otherwise congenial cats suddenly to seek sanctuary on the kitchen table or the record player, where they scratch, bite, gnaw, and indicate by so doing that the only good flea is a dead flea. What bugs me most (if you'll excuse the expression), they then glare at us as if to say, "So what are you going to do about it?"

When the cats aren't busily engaged in dislodging a flea, they are busily engaged in shedding. If you'll excuse the digression, our cats don't go in for your common everyday indiscriminate releasing of cat hair. Oh, no. *Their* hair must make a difference. White on white, of course, would be a complete waste of cat hair. White Cat will go for days without turning loose a single hair, waiting for me to toss my blue flannel jacket carelessly over the arm of the sofa, or for a visitor to sit down foolishly wearing a black wool dress. It's at these opportune times that White Cat goes for complete baldness. And purrs loudest.

Now don't get the idea that we are allowing fleas to run rampant in our modest digs (if you'll excuse the pun). But killing fleas, as you may already have discovered, is not a piece of cake. In fact, it isn't even *close* to a piece of cake. Especially if the cats misconstrue your efforts as an attempt to do away with them and not the fleas. As our cats do.

We have unwisely blown a sizable portion of our retirement kitty (I'm sorry) on various cans of flea and tick "killers." Directions call for us to "apply directly to animals along the back, under forelegs, and other areas except for private parts (to put it more delicately than the directions put it). Part hair to contact skin and insure good cover...apply until hair is thoroughly moist."

Our cats allow us to part their hair, no problem there. But that's it. One spray from the can and they are halfway to the next county. They aren't going to be knocked off with that stuff; no way.

After running them down and reestablishing congeniality, our next strategy is to turn our backs, spray some of that stuff on our hands, and rub our hands over their backs. We never do get to their forelegs. One whiff and they disappear for the next two days.

With the cats away, the fleas have no alternative but to chum up with the nice people who furnished the cats in the first place. Having taken advantage of the cats' absence to spray the floors, the sofa, the chair seats, the bookcases, and the ceilings, we now find these little demons crawling on us. And there's nothing worse than a flea with wet feet climbing up your bare leg.

Attempting to rub the rascals to death is another futile effort. After rubbing until your skin is raw, you raise your thumb to view the remains, only to find (I'm guessing at this) that the flea is now 40 feet away laughing its fool head off.

Why don't you buy flea collars? I can hear you thinking. And why don't I buy Aunt Nellie a ten-speed wheelchair? It

Playing Leapfrog with Porcupines

would make as much sense. Besides, flea collars would chafe our necks.

Oh, we have tried collars on the cats. For years we inaugurated each flea season by installing these devices. How the fleas loved them. They would come from all corners of the cats to get their aerobic exercises by frolicking on these new attractions.

Where we made our mistake was in fastening the collars around the cats' necks. To kill a flea with a flea collar you must first position the flea upon a hard, smooth surface (no small trick in itself), then bring the collar down smartly across the surface of the flea.

Though seldom fatal—and the flea won't hang around for a second try—this course of action at least offers the hint that he might not be welcome. Should the course also break a few ribs, or rupture his spleen, so much the better, as the little critter's jumping range would be restricted to something less than 40 feet. Until he heals, that is.

So...what's the final solution? There isn't one. But that doesn't stop us from blowing the last dime of the cat budget at Wal-Mart for a three-can set of "Foggers."

Although the guarantee on these cans doesn't come right out and claim that the fog will kill fleas, cockroaches, chiggers, horseflies, Japanese beetles, tsetse flies, and so on, at least you are given the impression that it will make these not-wanteds pretty darn sick—headaches, nausea, diarrhea, that sort of thing.

Directions are simple: Remove the cats from the house; remove the spouse, place the foggers in areas where flea traffic is heaviest (Friday afternoon is best), push down on the button, and remove yourself.

Three hours later, open the doors, turn on the fans, vacuum the flea sufferers off the carpets, and let the cats reenter the house. The fleas still residing on the cats will joyously jump off and beget a whole new colony.

As Jonathan Swift so properly put it:

Maynard Good Stoddard

> *So, naturalists observe, a flea*
> *Hath smaller fleas that on him prey;*
> *And these have smaller fleas that bite 'em;*
> *And so proceed* ad infinitum.

And as I, though perhaps not so properly, observe: The only thing that can be said for fleas is, instead of making us dread the advent of cold weather, fleas at least make us grateful for its return...because they have all gone to Miami for the winter.

Chapter 4

WHEN THE DOG BITES

Does anyone out there know the dates of this year's National Dog Bite Prevention Week? I fear it may already be history, as last year it fell on the week of June 12 to 17. I still have the postcard the dog-bite people added to my important mail announcing those vital dates. Anyway, we can at least pick up a few pointers from last year's card.

"More than two million dog bites are reported each year in the United States," we read. "It's a problem for everyone—not just the 2,700 letter carriers who were bitten last year." The card includes a list of tips on "How to avoid being bitten." Which leads me to ask, "Where were those tips when I needed them?"

Not that I ever served my country as a letter carrier, but for several years (it seemed longer), I risked life, limb, and the seat of my pants daily as a door-to-door representative of the Realsilk Hosiery Mills. In this capacity I served as fair game for all the kids within a three-block area, not to mention bulldogs with teeth too long for their mouths and nearsighted mutts that had trouble distinguishing between a salesman's leg and a fire hydrant.

The traffic at times became so stressful that I would risk having a door slammed on my foot just to get in somewhere out of the dogs and the kids. If I should happen to make a sale, so much the better.

An endangered species for years, the door-to-door salesman by now may be extinct. But in case a few hardy souls are still limping down the street, I may keep their species viable by reviving an experience or two from my own "dog days" and adding a tip or two from the dog-bite prevention card.

One of those tips goes something like this. In fact, it goes exactly like this. "If a dog threatens you, don't scream. Avoid eye contact, try to remain motionless until the dog leaves, then back away slowly until the dog is out of sight."

Easy for them to say. But the only occasions upon which I remained motionless were those occasions upon which I fainted. Otherwise, I preceded the dog well into the next block and, on more than one occasion, underwent the awkwardness of walking to the nearest bus stop holding my sample case over my tattered stern section.

Then there were dogs fresh from obedience school who had gotten an A in Deception 101.

If you are not among the extinct, and your territory covers lower Michigan, and you are working the road running west out of Columbiaville, and you make a call at the house on the north side of the road just before it dead-ends, I have a tip that may save you a stitch or two.

If the dog residing here hasn't gone to his reward (eternally treed by a cat would be appropriate), he will rise from the welcome mat greeting you like a long-lost master returning home with a sample case stuffed with T-bones, medium rare. Bouncing confidently up the steps, you'll give him a pat on the head, pronounce him "Good boy" and "Nice doggie," and ring the doorbell. Not until the "lady" of the house tells you to get lost and you pick up your sample case does it penetrate the dog's thick skull that you are stealing something.

Too late for me—but I hope not for you—I read on the dog-bite prevention card: "Don't run past a dog. The dog's natural instinct is to chase and catch prey." And by golly, the card is right.

Though I sat gingerly for the next two days, the incident failed to make as deep an impression on my mind. Would you believe—yes, I suppose you would—the next time I worked that area I called at that same house, patted that same dog, got that same command from that "lady," and not until turning to leave did it penetrate my thick skull. "Hey, this is the dog that..." Too late. His teeth were already embedded in the calf of my leg. For all I know, my sample case may still be there.

Playing Leapfrog with Porcupines

Now let us back up a sec. The people promoting dog-bite prevention suggest that you "always let a dog see and sniff you before you pet the animal." (How you can pet an animal that doesn't see you is the dog-bite people's own little secret.) Their advice apparently applies to dogs you contact on the street. What the prevention people fail to consider is that dogs are on the street for one of two reasons. Either they have been kicked out of the house or they haven't had a house to be kicked out of.

In case number one, the dog is looking for a kid carelessly holding a Burger King "Whopper." In case number two, the dog is seeking affection. It's case number two that concerns us.

You are walking down the street (unless there's a sidewalk), hoping to spot a house that might indicate the owners are desperate for your merchandise. (Such houses are not as easy to spot as you might think.) And here comes a Russian wolfhound whose mother had been crossed, double-crossed, more than likely—by a Great Dane. Let the dog see you and sniff you, right?

The dog sees you, no problem there. But sniffing is not on his mind.

All he wants to do is plant his big fat feet upon your shoulders and begin licking your face, his breath a dead giveaway that he has come directly from surfing the landfill. I know what I'm talking about.

The door-to-door salesman is now left with two options: Number one, he can go home and change clothes; number two, he can continue making calls, facing the ignominy of potential customers taking one sniff of the dog's deposit on his shoulders and throwing open a window.

The card's final warning has to do with "approaching a strange dog, especially one that's tied or confined."

I take you now to Birk Street (dubbed "Birth Street" because of the rabble of kids per house), Ann Arbor, Michigan. I am still trying to resocket my left hip joint after punching a "hot doorbell" —that's a doorbell which the fun-loving owner has wired to produce at least 1,500 volts of electricity whenever he sees a salesman approaching—and being knocked backwards down a flight of porch steps.

But before I can regain flight speed, five kids of this house, having exhausted their supply of frozen snowballs, emerge from behind a snow fort and escort me reluctantly toward the front door. Before reaching that sanctuary, however, the Hound of the Baskervilles with a thyroid condition comes charging around the corner of the house obviously with more in mind than sniffing this beleaguered stranger.

Giving credit where credit is limited, the mother of this brood charges out the front door to confine the slobbering beast. And while she is confining him—I'm not kidding—the littlest man of the family slips around and bites me in the leg.

I now take you back to the original question. Remember the original question? My reason for wanting to know the dates of this year's Dog Bite Prevention Week has to do with last year's card listing a number of suggestions on "How to be a responsible dog owner."

If the door-to-door salesman hasn't already been wiped out and I'm barking up the wrong tree, I have a few suggestions of my own I would like to present to the committee handling this section of dog-bite prevention.

- Yell "Bad dog!" every time your mongrel bites a salesman upon his departure (or anywhere else, for that matter). The beast may eventually learn to attack when the salesman approaches, giving him a running chance.
- Cut the voltage on the "hot doorbell" to a reasonable 500 volts. Although flat on his back, the victim might still remain on the porch rather than down the steps.
- Check obedience schools for one that teaches affection-starved dogs to greet strangers with a lick on the hand instead of by the planting of both feet on the shoulder.

- In addition to confining your dog when the door-to-door salesman nears your front door, the species might remain viable if you will extend your compassion also to confining your kid with the overbite.

Stuff like that.

Chapter 5

WOULDN'T THIS FROST YA!

If, at this very minute, I was to confront my dear wife—who shall be nameless, for reasons soon to become apparent—and ask her if our checkbook balance stands closer to $5.00 or $5,000 (that $5,000 being a joke, of course), her studied answer would be, "Hmmm?"

Now, I love my wife as much as the next man. Loves his wife, perhaps I should add. But she doesn't have the slightest clue of where we stand assetwise because I'm the one who pays the monthly bills. I'm the one who writes the checks...and writes the checks...and writes the checks. Such as this current one for the electric bill. ("Current" one. "Electric" bill. Get it?)

There are a number of reasons why the electric bill leads the parade in sapping our assets to the red-ink stage every 30 days.

Reason No. 1: This woman I took for better or worse keeps the refrigerator motor running full tilt by holding the door open until her eyebrows frost and the furnace fires up. Sometimes it's for downsizing. She'll dump last week's spinach-and-gizzard casserole remains into a smaller container, saving upwards of one entire linear inch of space in the exchange.

Other times, it is merely to browse. "Hmm," she'll say, "that must be the Hungarian goulash from last Thursday. I must remember to fry it for Maynard's breakfast tomorrow." Only yesterday I heard her say, "That looks like coleslaw in the Jell-O. I wonder how that got in there."

Now and then she'll keep the door open for a leisurely game of "refrigerator checkers." With my eyebrows frosting on the far side of the kitchen, she will move this dish over to that empty space, then jump a dish over that dish and move the jumped dish to a lower shelf, from where it will have to work its way up again. Some of these dishes have mold on the outside.

Playing Leapfrog with Porcupines

My setting an example of refrigerator alacrity has been a waste of time. If I'm taking out, I know exactly what I want and where it is before going in. Putting in, I can stick the stuff in and slam the door before the motor knows I'm there. My best time for a dish of coleslaw and bowl of Jell-O is two seconds flat.

But it's not only the fridge that's freezing any hope of our checking account arriving one day at that elusive $5,000 mark. There's also the thermostat—offering a temperature range from 50 to (unfortunately) 100—that regulates the furnace beneath the livingroom floor. Until I can get my hackles up to the point where I will jerk the contraption out of the wall, roots and all, solvency remains a lost cause.

In all fairness (which is a switch, I can hear you saying), the dollar drainage here may not be entirely the fault of you-and-I-know-who. Perhaps due to a prenatal temperamental problem of some sort, the nurses must have packed her in ice cubes at birth. And now, by golly, she's going to make up for it.

This means that the temperature in our humble hovel must be maintained at a paint-blistering setting near the top. Let me try to sneak the needle down to the "comfort zone," and the other occupant can be found buried beneath a sweater, a jacket, and the afghan, chattering, "Are we out of fuel?"

So back it goes, with the first occupant spending his indwelling hours stripped to the waist and sweating like the proverbial steer in a cornfield.

Perhaps I should explain right here—if I'm not too late—about my hemoglobin. In simple terms, hemoglobin is "the oxygen-bearing, iron-containing, conjugated protein in vertebrate red blood cells, consisting of about 6 percent heme and 94 percent globin and having as a typical formula ($C_{738}H_{1166}FeN_{203}O_{208}S_2)_4$." But don't take my word for it.

Anyway, the temperature problem keeps coming up because my hemes hover around the 10 mark, and my globins are somewhere in the neighborhood of 108. (I know. That gives me a hemoglobin rating of 118, but that's the way it is.) Dear wife, on the other hand, must have no more than a single heme, and her globins register closer to zero. Thus I don't complain of the cold until my dentures begin to ache and she wears mittens to handle the silverware.

You might think that bedtime would give the watt-hour meter some relief from its hectic daily pace. We have finished the bedtime reading, I by the rays coming through our window from the security light, she by a lamp holding a bulb of 50-100-150 wattage (no need to point out which two of the three numbers remain in their virgin state); the telephone (we'll get to that) lies quietly in its cradle; and the red light no longer glows on the kitchen range (remind me to get to that, too). The only excuse the meter wheel now has for not nodding off itself is the lighted dial on the digital clock perched on the cedar chest. Right?

Sorry. You have overlooked the electric blanket with dual controls, a Christmas gift from *her* to *me* four years ago. My control has yet to be turned on. Her control, except during the halcyon months of July and August, has yet to be turned off. And has she ever tried the "low" or "medium" setting? Fat chance. From beddown to bedup, it's set ALL THE WAY! Why her side of the bed hasn't caught fire by this time is little short of a miracle.

In addition to the expense of the voltage, what burns me up is that if one of my temperate feet should happen to stray over into her torrid zone during the midnight hours, you'd think I had dumped a load of frozen catfish on her. By the time I get her back into bed, I'm at full alert. And since I'm alert, what do I hear?

"How about turning up the heat?"

If you haven't gone outside to take a breath of fresh air by this time, there are a few more things apropos of this mess.

The teakettle stays hot all day. No telling when someone might be popping in (like the meter reader, say, awarding us for being User of the Month) and dying for a spot of tea.

Now this may be slightly beside the point, not that it has ever stopped me before, but I write letters. She telephones. My

Playing Leapfrog with Porcupines

monthly postage bill runs .64. If her telephone bill is less than $70, I have this crazy thought that we have saved money. My two letters are usually fresh attempts to raise cash. She will talk to one of our daughters for a half hour, regardless of said daughter coming tomorrow for a three-day visit.

She will leave the vacuum cleaner on for the full half hour that she's talking. I turn off the engine of my big red 11-horse Murray riding mower to smooth a mole mound directly in its path.

I could go on. But I have a feeling that this already may result in my having to turn on my electric blanket for the first time.

Besides, I already know what you are thinking. No, I don't mean getting her to take a vow of poverty. I've tried that. You are thinking, *Why doesn't this dummy wake up and turn the checkbook over to Lois for a couple of months and let her write the checks?* (Now you've done it!) *Once she sees the results of her extravagance in black and white, he'll have a completely changed woman on his hands.* (You said it, I didn't.)

Oh yeah! We may be headed for bankruptcy, buddy, but I'm not ripe for the loony bin. Not yet, anyway. Besides, she can already see the results of her monthly luxuries in black and white by looking on the refrigerator door, where I paste the bills.

Which reminds me. Somewhere I read of a refrigerator with a see-through glass door. Hmm...it would at least be a start.

Chapter 6

COUNTRY LIVING—AS IT'S CALLED

I'm afraid my dear wife has been spending too much time under the hair dryer. The result has been her half-baked idea of moving from our snug apartment in Indianapolis to this...this *house,* for want of a better word (the word "hovel" now comes to mind), on a windswept hill in Sweet Owen County. Where once the only demand upon my physical output was painting the patio birdbath once a year, I now am trying to avoid a second hernia.

Our move occurred, appropriately, on April Fools' Day. The coincidence first came to light after I had hauled the last of our worldly possessions out of the U-Haul and asked for a drink. Water would do.

"Oh, did you forget?" trilled my rustic wife, who much prefers moving to dusting. "Our drinking water comes from a flowing well only half a mile down old Route 67. Fresh, pure water right out of the ground. No more of that treated city stuff for us. Won't that be great!"

No doubt about it. If slaloming down a potholed road and filling gallon milk jugs with this pastoral Perrier can be called great, we'd be having a ball.

Thankfully, I wasn't required to haul water for the "shower," a spigoted oil drum that the clever former owner had mounted on a two-by-four tripod and hidden behind the root cellar entrance. Water for this Taj Mahal luxury I could haul up from the cistern just off the back porch.

This stuff collected from drainage off the roof fell somewhat short of the fresh, pure water right out of the ground. About the only thing going for it was that it was wet. Unless you could count a belly-up spider or two in each bucket, sometimes a fatally exhausted garter snake, and on one occasion a clumsy chipmunk. After straining, the remaining residue would be dumped into the oil drum to be warmed by the sun, a duty the

Playing Leapfrog with Porcupines

sun often shirked. Gail Abrell, our neighbor in the valley, once confided that his family could tell whenever I showered on cloudy days because they could hear me scream.

Now I'll be the first—make that the second—to point out that when it comes to shortcomings in the manual arts, I come up among the shortest. If I can get the "+" and "-" ends of batteries installed in a flashlight in their correct order, that's about it. I long ago gave up trying to install a roll of toilet paper on the holder so it wouldn't go rolling across the floor for the next customer.

However, while putting up the hammock—my No. 1 priority on this particular day—my dear wife happened to overhear me yelling, "The human system was not geared to jump directly from painting a birdbath to overhauling a five-room landfill. The stress could easily bring on a case of shingles, if not the whole roof."

"The rooms need more light," she said, deeply concerned.

"No problem," I told her. "When I get out of the hammock, I'll upgrade the lightbulbs."

"What I had in mind," she said with a patronizing smile, having misinterpreted my reply as a weak joke, "was replacing those narrow windows and doors with picture windows and patio doors."

"Me?"

"You," she said, folding up the hammock.

"And how does the title of Widow Stoddard sound to you?" I whined.

Actually, thanks to earlier efforts by the termites, I could have removed the first window casing with nothing more than a fingernail file. The hitch was, *my* efforts happened to coincide with the annual convention of the Federated Hornets of Sweet Owen County, and I had just removed the entrance to their meeting place.

Our ad in the Spencer *Evening World* read: "Old doors and windows to be replaced. Man having good rapport with hornets preferred."

My next exercise in shortcomings involved what is known in the trade as "dropping the ceiling." To save heat, my dear wife explained.

What she failed to explain was how people in the trade manage to keep the counfounded ceiling tile from dropping to the floor from the metal rails that took me three days to suspend from the one-by-twos that required another three days to nail to the old ceiling.

On day eight (I don't labor on Sundays), dear wife stuck her head in from the safety of the doorway and suggested I leave the ceiling dropping to the door and window person and take up some other improvement. Like digging a hole beneath the living room to accommodate a floor furnace. Which would not have been among my top ten choices.

Not when the—what the heck, let's call it a house—rests not upon a foundation but flat out on the ground. Especially not when the terra firma has the ideal firma required for the manufacture of bowling balls. And definitely not when the bowling clay gives way to limestone only three feet below the surface.

Arriving finally at this strata, this allowed me three feet of space to swing the pickax from a kneeling position and bury the top pick in the timber supporting the living room. Working it loose and bringing the bottom pick down on the limestone would knock out a flake—oh, sometimes as large as a quarter. How the two gentlemen from Sears managed to conceal their admiration for my five weeks of effort can probably be traced to jealousy. But not once during the four days they laid on their respective backs installing the furnace did they mention it.

Nothing left for me now but to locate the hammock and let my spinal column work its way to perpendicular. Right?

Not in Sweet Owen County, buddy. According to the building code, an oil furnace without an outside chimney constitutes a no-no. You either put up a chimney or you call Sears and ask the two gentlemen to come back and wrestle their furnace out of the hole. I decided to go the chimney route.

Playing Leapfrog with Porcupines

Two long weeks and two days later, the first chimney blocks rose above the eaves, and I said to myself, "If the fumes come this far, surely they'll know the direction from here on." I brought out my dear wife to extend the credit where credit certainly was overdue.

After surveying in silence this masterpiece of masonry for some time (too awed to speak, I assumed), she finally managed to comment, "Makes the Leaning Tower of Pisa look kinda sick, doesn't it?"

"If you'll recall," I haughtily reminded her, "the wind has been blowing pretty hard most of the time I've been masoning." She had no reply.

Now, just for fun, how long would you say an apartment-pampered woman will wait before beginning her campaign for running water (over and above that from the kitchen ceiling during a rainstorm, that is)? If your answer is two months, you're in the ballpark. My argument that we clean the cistern and fill it with water delivered from Spencer didn't hold water, you might say. (I wouldn't say it, but you might.)

The local well driller agreed to drill a well at nine dollars a foot. Checking with Gail Abrell, our neighbor down the hill, and learning that their well was only 26 feet, I told the driller to come on up.

Have you ever stood at your $758 picture window in the living room and witnessed ten-foot pipes being driven into the firma, one after the other, to the drilling machine's rhythmic dirge, "nine dollars a foot...nine dollars a foot...nine dollars a foot?" It's not a pretty picture, definitely not a soothing sound.

On day four, the head driller came to the window joyfully waiving three fingers. Taking this to mean they had drilled 300 feet of pipe into the ground, I began looking for a convenient place to pass out. Then I heard him shout that they had struck a vein producing three gallons of water a minute— "at only 248 feet!" A neat savings of 52 feet. What a relief!

Of course, there was still the numbing expense of installing a jet pump at the bottom of the well to force water to the surface. And what good is running water if you don't have something to run it to? Like a hot-water heater, a holding tank, a hydrant, and stuff like that? My motion that we run the water into the mounted oil drum never came to a vote. Instead, by a vote of one to one, we added a bathroom to this...this *house.*

And as long as we were adding on, why not add on enough to accommodate a sewing room and two closets for her, one for him? And while we were at it, how about making the concrete slab large enough for a patio—with a love seat, in case we were still on speaking terms by the time this outgo had stopped going out?

The front porch, where once we fed our little feathered friends, has now been enclosed with 12 windows at $68 per window. Upon which our little feathered friends are beginning to bash their little feathered brains out because of lack of warning strips.

The root cellar that once served as a wading pool after a heavy rain is now emptied automatically by means of a sump pump, thanks to the one of us having the shorter legs. And those dirt walls were so—so *dirty.* Why not have old hubby risk a second hernia by hauling up rocks from the creek bed and cementing them in place for a wall "that will last and last"? (Longer than old hubby will last, that's for sure). By now, I know every one of those rocks by name. And the names I call them, you wouldn't want to know.)

Today, my duties having been reduced to no more than mowing two acres of what we stubbornly claim as a lawn on a grade of 30 degrees, and digging out elm tree stumps occupying the exact spot that my dear wife has chosen for her rock garden (with guess-who furnishing the rocks), she has hit upon what she considers to be the greatest idea since Sir Isaac Newton got beaned by a Red Delicious.

Our daughter Shari, and grandson, Kris, having moved from Sweet Owen County to hot and humid Columbia, South Carolina, why not sell our view (remember our view?) and move on down? Not in the city, especially. Just a little place we can continue to enjoy country living.

Chapter 7

LOCK, STOCK, BARREL, AND BLUING

Teenagers today wouldn't be going around shooting other teenagers—or even people—if they had owned a BB gun at age six or eight. I myself owned a BB gun at age six, maybe eight, somewhere in that vicinity and I haven't touched a gun since. You couldn't pay me to touch a gun. I hate guns. You want to know why? Let me tell you.

At age six, possibly eight, I saw this ad: it must have been in the *Breeder's Gazette* because that was the only publication coming to our house (except for *The Saturday Evening Post*, of course—retailing then for five cents). The ad promised that if I sold a "gross" of bluing, this company would send me a BB gun ABSOLUTELY FREE.

I didn't know what a "gross" meant, much less anything about bluing, but I knew BB guns, and I sure wanted one. Especially an absolutely free one. So I managed to fill out the coupon, sneak an envelope and a two-cent stamp (I must have been eight), and slip the envelope into our mailbox on my walk to school the next morning.

The day the bluing arrived turned into the longest day I had spent to date. Upon regaining her faculty of speech after opening the package, my previously conservative, Pennsylvania-Dutch mother cried out, "Why on God's green earth would you order 144 packages of bluing!"

One hundred and forty-four. So *that* was a gross.

"I couldn't use 144 packages of bluing if I was doing laundry for the Third Army," she moaned, as the stuff continued to erupt from the cardboard carton and slither across the kitchen table.

"You don't have to use it," I said, with my one and only chuckle of the day. "I'm going to sell it and get a BB gun absolutely free."

Playing Leapfrog with Porcupines

To divert her attention from the quantity, and acquire ammunition for my sales pitch, I brightly asked, "What's the stuff for?"

With a sign of resignation, she explained that mothers added bluing to the washing machine water to make white clothes whiter.

"You make white clothes whiter by adding bluing?" I repeated. "I'd think you'd use whiting for white clothes and bluing for blue clothes to make them bluer."

She just stared at me. Mother used to stare at me a lot when I was six or eight, or whatever.

Now that I remember it, the longest day might have been the following day. It being Saturday, I planned on covering the entire territory of Richfield Center (Michigan, that is), consisting of maybe 20 houses, by nightfall—if the merchandise lasted that long, of course.

Armed with my sales talk ("How about some bluing to stick in your washing machine to make your white clothes whiter?") and toting my stock in a canvas bag previously used as a nosebag for our horse, I set off to confront my first prospect. This would be Mrs. Cross, wife of the blacksmith, our next-door neighbor.

Unfortunately, I had no sooner mounted the porch steps than I heard Mrs. Cross yell to Mr. Cross that he wasn't fit to shoe a horse. So I decided that she would not be in the mood to buy bluing then. I passed up the Garrison house because all five of the boys would be mad at me for getting a BB gun just for selling bluing.

Approaching the Bentleys, I remembered barely in time that we had ripped the seam of their downspout with a Giant Cracker while celebrating last year's Fourth of July. The Reigles had clothes on the line, the white things looking so white I knew that Mrs. Reigle had all the bluing she needed.

This brought me to my Aunt Blanche's house. She took one package. My dear mother took the other 143. Although not quite clear on what it was for, dear old Dad made out the check, and I sent it off on Monday morning.

Maynard Good Stoddard

I waited. And waited. And kept on waiting. Fall turned to winter; spring, as it often did in those days, slowly followed. Still no gun. On my daily trips to the mailbox now, however, I began to notice that melting snow was revealing more and more of a strip of brown paper beneath the branches of the Christmas tree we had tossed into the ditch. Curiosity getting the better of me, I stopped one day to investigate.

How long my gun might have been lying there, I didn't bother to speculate. The well-deserved reward for my labors I now held in my eager little mitts. That's all that mattered.

Ignoring the enclosed directions (a habit I have maintained to this day), 500 BBs having been included in the package, I unscrewed the end of the barrel, dumped in the full 500, replaced the barrel cap, and headed for the chicken house, favorite hangout for sparrows looking for stray kernels of wheat.

Sure enough, on a roost sat a lone pushover. I closed the door. It flitted to a closed window, foolishly clinging to the frame. I raised my trusty weapon, squinted along the twin sights until it came dead center. With the anticipation Teddy Roosevelt must have experienced bagging his first buffalo, I pulled the trigger.

Had only a single BB ejected from the barrel, the bird might have survived. But even a bald eagle would have had a hard time prolonging its life under a barrage of all 500, including the magazine itself. An autopsy confirmed that not a single BB had penetrated the epidermis, leaving me to conclude that marksmanship had played little part in the bird's demise. The poor thing had simply been weighted to death.

I never before had held a bird in my hand. I never knew that a sparrow would weigh no more than a marshmallow, that its feathers could be so soft, its markings so precise. I never knew that I could feel so guilty.

Tradition, of course, called for a hunter to mount his first trophy proudly above the mantel. Not this hunter. This hunter would lay out his little feathered trophy in a matchbox, place a

Playing Leapfrog with Porcupines

few kernels of wheat near its partly opened beak, and bury the box, secretly, on the sunny side of the chicken house.

I would never shoot at a live target again.

Had I been smart for my age of six or eight, or whatever, I would have buried the BB gun alongside the matchbox. But I wasn't. And I didn't. And the absolutely free firearm would on two more occasions cause me to regret not being smart for my age of six or eight, or whatever.

Belatedly checking the instruction sheet, I saw the BBS went into the magazine, not the barrel, dummy. It had a capacity of 50, not 500. Now, when shooting at unlive targets such as tin cans or the headlamp on brother Meryl's bicycle (I never had a bicycle), a pull on the trigger would release but the required single BB. The problem now was in coaxing that single BB to appear.

If I held the gun at the slightest upward angle, the shooting mechanism had all it could do making the BB clear the end of the barrel. Only by pointing the gun downward would a shot come out with any show of enthusiasm. In desperation, I finally took the problem to dear old Dad.

Now, my Dad was not what you could call mechanically inclined. The only time he attempted to clean the spark plugs from our Model T, he alertly noticed the gap between the points. "No wonder she wasn't hitting on all four," we heard him mutter as he took a pair of pliers and expertly pinched the points together. When she then hit on exactly zero, Dad had to call on Bill Williams, our local mechanic, who returned the points to their proper spacing.

So why would I refer the sorry condition of my BB gun to a man who couldn't clean spark plugs? Because a man who couldn't clean spark plugs would sooner buy a new gun than tamper with a mechanism that would discharge a BB only at a downward angle. With this in mind, one seemingly favorable evening, I invited dear old Dad to accompany me outside for the all-important demonstration.

Cocking the gun and pointing it indiscriminately upward, and hoping to make my point more dramatic by catching the BB in my hand as it dribbled from the barrel, I pulled the trigger.

It would be the only time in its short life that the gun ejected a shot with a velocity beyond the capability of human eyesight. Human eyesight, unfortunately, had no trouble observing the unbelievable hole the BB had ripped in the eave trough directly above the entrance to our porch.

My dad only stared at me. He never stared at me as much as Mother stared at me, but sometimes he stared longer. This was one of those times.

The gun would betray me one more time before I finally relegated it to the attic to rust in peace.

You've heard of the "shot heard 'round the world"? This wasn't it, but surely it had been heard 'round Richfield Center, if not Puptown and even Henpeck, eight miles to the northeast.

My brother, Meryl, owned a .22 rifle (which he would never let me shoot), and I had this lousy BB gun. Thinking to even the score on this otherwise peaceful sunny afternoon, I liberated one of his live shells, with the idea of exploding it by inserting the bullet part in a hole in one of Mother's clothesline posts and hitting the cap of the shell with a hammer. (I had brighter ideas than that at age six or eight, or whatever, although none come to mind at the moment.)

Anyway, what happened was, when the shell didn't explode at the first whack, I kept whacking at it until I'd driven the cap flush with the post. With it still intact, I came up with an idea dumber yet. I would get my untrustworthy BB gun, position the hole in the barrel end against the shell cap in and post, and WHAMO!

The least I can say for the idea is, it worked. The shell not only exploded, it also ripped out a slab of the post that, having no other place to go, slapped me squarely in the face.

You talk about a pair of lips that would put a duckbill platypus to shame; I had them. I would have them for a week.

Playing Leapfrog with Porcupines

My two black eyes would require two additional weeks before finally turning an even more ugly orange.

As for trying to explain to dear old Mom and Dad that the blame lay with my velocity-impaired BB gun, forget it. This would be the first time, to my recollection, that they both stared at me in unison.

Looking back, as I'm more inclined to do these days, my BB gun trauma served three purposes. Not only did I swear off firearms for life; not only would today's kids of six or eight, or whatever, possibly follow suit; but what a wonderful feeling I had knowing that my dear mother would be spared the worry of running short of bluing for the rest of her life, if not longer.

Chapter 8

CROSS WORDS

We were no more than five paces into our power walk this morning when my dear wife turned up the collar of her jacket and said, "The wind is colder than it looks."

Though you may question the rationality of this remark, it didn't affect me. I have been immune to her wayward way with words for more years than you would believe.

The truth is (strange as this may sound), I had a pretty good start on this immunity before ever leaving home. My Pennsylvania Dutch mother once called out to me, "I can't come right now; my arms are knee-deep in dishwater." She also complained that she could "walk across the room without a stitch on and your father would never notice what I was wearing."

All of which pales next to the man, not long off the boat, who came into my dad's country grocery store to ask for "an empty barrel of flour to make a hencoop for my dog."

The abuse of language is not our topic for today, however. What currently is sapping my will to live concerns my dear wife's cavalier approach to the daily crossword puzzle in the *Indianapolis Star*.

Before you ask, I'll tell you what business it is of mine: I get the puzzle after she has given up on it. I, being the smarter of the two (this is off the record, of course), am left to fill in the blanks where her mind has gone blank. This would be fun and games were it not for her mind having gone blank on the squares she has already filled in.

Take a puzzle...go ahead, any puzzle. OK, you have picked September 5, 1992. Now remember, this is y*our* choice, not mine.

Where Mrs. Roget took her first flight of fancy was by filling in the five spaces calling for "River through Rome" with the five letters T-I-G-E-R. Didn't it fit? It did. Were not the "T"

Playing Leapfrog with Porcupines

and "R" already in their proper places? They were, so why not leave well enough alone and go merrily on your way? Why not leave the little matter of the "G" in T-I-G-E-R, causing the four-letter word for "Proficiently" to come out A-G-L-E to our successor?

If you can find the word "agle" in your dictionary, gentle reader, your dictionary serves you more agle than mine serves me.

Any person in her right mind, or a reasonable facsimile, would have at this point put her pencil on hold and asked herself, "Could I possibly have made a sight blunder in a preceding word?" Then there are minds that will accept the word A-G-L-E to be an abbreviation of "agility", and if "agility" and proficiently" aren't synonyms, then someone is out in left field without his glove. One can rectify such logic only by prayer and fasting.

By changing the river through Rome from T-I-G-E-R to T-I-B-E-R, the word for "proficiently" now became A-B-L-E rather than A-G-L-E—certainly an improvement, but still no cigar. The cigar would have to wait while I puzzled over the five letters for "Secure a boat," for which my dear wife had chosen B-E-L-I-E.

Now I ask you, who this side of Bellevue would ever yell out, "Hey you on the dock, would you mind helping me belie my boat?"

After altering B-E-L-I-E to B-E-L-A-Y, the word A-B-L-E became A-B-L-Y, and the word for "proficiently" was laid at last to rest.

Filling the five spaces across with S-H-U-T-S for "Closes" appears to be the work of a person rowing with both oars, right? The two S's being already in place, wouldn't it be charitable to say that two out of five is not bad? A baseball player getting two out of five would be hitting .400, for which we would have to go back to Ted Williams for such a record. However, two out of five in crossword puzzling leaves much to be desired.

Maynard Good Stoddard

For one thing to be desired, the middle three letters, H-U-T, cause the three words down to come out B-H-E-D-S, D-E-U-N-T, and T-E-L-T-S. Upon checking the first of these household words, I find B-H-E-D-S to be my predecessor's synonym for "Brews." If you haven't guzzled a stein of good old bheds, brother, you haven't lived. Not until I had changed "Closes" from S-H-U-T-S to S-E-A-L-S and made "Clams" S-T-E-A-M-E-R-S rather than S-T-E-A-M-E-D-S did "Brews" finally end up B-E-E-R-S.

I could go on—and if you have nothing better to do, I will. When one is in as much trouble as I am already, what's another cold dinner or another night on the old couch?

The four spaces for "Meditate" she had filled with the four letters P-O-S-E. Was my dear wife, in the words of Ann Landers, "a few sandwiches short of a picnic"? The only reasoning I could come up with was that when one meditates, one doesn't move around—one just sits there and poses.

Her P-L-A-N for "Intend," however, lay beyond my power of reasoning. Not until I had switched the letters for "intend" from P-L-A-N to M-E-A-N did "meditate" come out M-U-S-E rather than P-O-S-E. The switch also improved the spelling of A-D-O-L-T-E-R-A-T-E to A-D-U-L-T-E-R-A-T-E.

On the brighter side, of the 64 words across and the 54 down, Mrs. Roget had screwed up but 11. I'm sure she would insist, without asking, that 11 out of 118 borders on genius.

One the darker side, if I am to retain my equilibrium, I may have to lay out another $109 per year for a second subscription to the *Indianapolis Star* to get my very own unsullied puzzle. Darker still is the thought that my dear wife's genes for working crossword puzzles may have already flowed into the veins (or wherever genes flow) of the third generation.

I can already hear little Stephanie respond to a question from her third-grade teacher: "I'm not sure—could I have a minute to pose on it?"

Playing Leapfrog with Porcupines

You'll have to excuse me now. Dear wife just opened my dungeon door to ask if I knew a seven-letter word for "Bird sanctuary." I told her C-R-O-W-B-A-R". She went away delighted.

I'm thinking of going fishing for the rest of the day.

Chapter 9

HAPPY 58th

The main reason why my dear wife and I didn't celebrate our last (make that latest) wedding anniversary separately had to do with her getting her head shut in the patio door.

The way it happened, she had unwisely invited the neighbor's nondescript pup to come inside for the purpose of tongue-mopping the kitchen floor around the cats' dish. The task completed, dear wife had been unable to eject the little beast. Each time she tried, he would scoot back in before she could pull the door shut. After the fourth attempt, I volunteered to handle the door while she did the ejecting.

I still contend that she was at fault for reacting so slowly when the door closed - or would have closed, had her head not been in the way. She, of course, had to go running around holding her ears and making out as if I had half-killed her. But I could tell she was faking.

You know how tapping watermelon will reveal if it's ripe: p-i-n-g, it isn't; t-h-u-d-, it is. Dear wife's head had gone p-i-n-g, so I knew she wasn't hurt that bad. I also had a feeling that the incident would be costing me more than an apology.

"Anniversaries are meant to be celebrated only on the fives and the zeros," I gently explained. "So I don't believe this one qualifies."

"Rubbish!" she exclaimed. "The 58th is just as important as the 50th. Even more so, now that I think of it."

"Fifty-eighth! Seems more like the 59th. And now that *I* think of it, how about that trip to Hawaii a couple of weeks ago? It should count for something."

"We took that trip last June," she said. "Where've you been?"

It seems I have married a woman who at times has to check her driver's license to remember her name, but can reel off to the

Playing Leapfrog with Porcupines

day the last time hubby brought her flowers, complimented her cooking, or took her anywhere. Yet she has no compunction about buying a size "S" jacket at a yard sale in March and calling it my birthday gift. No matter that my birthday occurs in July. Or that I wear a size "L."

How about our cruise to Nova Scotia?" I persisted. "We could count that…"

We took that cruise in August of '93, for heaven's sake!" (See what I mean?)

"OK, OK. We'll dine at Ryan's Steak House instead of Hardee's and then take in a movie. How does that grab you?"

Releasing one ear, she used the shifty little hand to spread a colorful broadside across the kitchen table. "What I had in mind was more like ten days at this ocean-front efficiency in Myrtle Beach."

With a sickening feeling of resignation, I gazed down at photos of sand, surf, and sunshine, all adorned with lovely young maidens clad in little more than their suntanned epidermises. Or epidermi. Or whatever. The clincher was a shot of the "efficiency" that would allow us to eat "in" instead of "out," thus saving at least half the cost of such a fling. And with senior citizen discount, it might actually be cheaper than staying home. It says here.

To reach Myrtle Beach from Freedom, you have only to drive to Columbia, South Carolina, and make a hard left. Upon arriving at the ocean, stop; you are there. Where the efficiency might be is not this simple.

It's on Ocean Boulevard," my life's companion explains, opening the broadside and the following discussion.

"And how do we find Ocean Boulevard?"

"I'm taking a wild guess that it runs parallel to the ocean," she quipped.

"Are we on it now?"

"I wouldn't know."

"Is it too much to ask if you'd look at some street signs?…"

"Yes, we're on it."

"Are we headed in the right direction?"

"We're supposed to be going north—2800 North Ocean Blvd."

"Well, are we headed north?"

"I haven't the foggiest."

"Could you possibly check the house numbers to see if they go up or down?"

"They're all business places."

"And they don't have numbers?"

"I don't see any. Besides, it's getting dark. I'm not a cat, you know."

Stifling an instinctive answer, I drive until she finally breaks the chilly silence by announcing, "You might be interested in the fact that we are no longer on Ocean Boulevard."

"Not on!...For Pete's sake, how could you have gotten us off?"

"Me! You were the one who went straight on when the street branched. You obviously should have branched."

"Do you happen to recall which way it branched?"

"Toward the ocean, naturally. So I suggest you might try turning right at the next street."

So I try turning right at the next street...and hit a dead end.

"The next street, eh?"

"I meant the next through street, of course, not a cul-de-sac. You've turned onto a cul-de-sac."

"I know it's a cul-de-sac. I can't tell a dead-end street from a through street without your help."

"You don't seem to."

"I should have gone to Ryan's and a movie."

"It's not too late. Just drop me off and when I get home, we can exchange photos of our celebrations."

Tongue- and body-weary, we found our destination at 10:45 p.m. After lugging wife's four pieces of luggage up to the immaculate ocean-front efficiency, I walked out onto the balcony. One look at moonlight shimmering on the Atlantic and one listen to the white-maned surf racing along the beach, and I

Playing Leapfrog with Porcupines

knew I had lost another one. On the way back to the car for my single suitcase, I stopped to check out the kitchen-dining area where dear wife would be throwing up (make that preparing) our money-saving meals.

There would be no "efficiency" eating the first day, of course, as that day was the Biggie, number 58. We brunched at the eating arena in Myrtle Square Mall only a two-block walk away and dined by candlelight at a restaurant recommended as the area's finest. As long as we'd be feeding frugally at "home" for the remaining nine days, what the heck.

To cement our relationship further, I scoured the mall for an appropriate gift. I knew it had to be something beyond gold and short—very short—of diamond. That would eliminate tinfoil; dear wife doesn't chew gum anyway. But how about stainless steel? I asked myself. Getting no answer, I then suggested copper.

To be on the safe side, I finally had a salesgirl conceal under double wrap a stainless steel saucepan with copper bottom. (Lest there be confusion, the saucepan had the copper bottom.) As an ace in the hole, I also picked up a copper bracelet. And, purely for sentimental reasons, added a pot of gorgeous African violets.

Have you ever felt like something someone had ordered and forgot to call for? Let me tell you about it.

At the unwrapping ceremony, I learned that my dear wife already owned a one-quart stainless steel saucepan with copper bottom. She also had been trying to give away, without success, her overflow of African violets (indicating that those things breed like field mice).

"The copper bracelet is good for relieving arthritis," I pointed out, standing aside in case she began turning cartwheels.

"I don't have arthritis," she answered back.

"But should you come down with it, you'll be all set," I said, wishing that in place of a bracelet I'd given her a choker (just kidding, of course). What really saved the occasion, however, and incidentally saved me a few bucks, was my original anniversary card:

> "You've been my wife through thick and thin,
> And though thin for years you haven't been,
> You're still the apple of my eye
> And will be till the day I pass on." ("Die" sounded—
> so *final*.)

Actually (and I'd just as soon this went no further), I might not have gone all-out on the gifts and the dining high on the hog had it not been for the comforting thought that my bride of 58 years would be preparing our meals, practically cost free, for the remaining eight days. The thought of my one day becoming Chief Justice of the Supreme Court would be of equal validity.

Basic supplies at the mini-mart just up the street totaled $17.23. And at the Bagel Factory a block away, if we bought a dozen we got an extra bagel free—and you know me. We added cream cheese, of course. And as long as we were there, why not sample their morning menu—just this once?

After our second breakfast of rye bagels, we put a little zip in the meal by switching to blueberry bagels. Three breakfasts of blueberry bagels, and we switched to Harry's for breakfast. Harry's was just across the street from Uncle John's, where we had been partaking of dinners. Evidently having seen us daily walking past on our way to the mall for lunch, Uncle John had cunningly stuck his menu out where dear wife would stop and be induced.

Our big excitement on day six consisted of watching the gulls compete for $17.23 worth of basic supplies and the remaining bagels.

Anyway, to make a long story sickening (if I haven't already), the only dishes my dear wife washed during the entire ten days of celebrating number 58 at our ocean-front efficiency totaled two coffee cups and one knife for spreading cream cheese. Even the coffee was instant. In her defense, however, I hasten to point out that she had to perform the task of spreading the cream cheese and stirring the coffee for five days straight.

Playing Leapfrog with Porcupines

I still say we should have had an adjustment on our bill by sparing the culinary utilities and not wearing out the dishes. I might suggest it when we go back for number 59—unless I can talk you-know-who into Ryan's and a movie.

Chapter 10

TAKE MY HUSBAND...PLEASE!

The reason I feel compelled to write "my side" of the story is because my lesser half, Maynard, just tried to run me down with his big red 11-horse Murray riding mower.

When I came out from behind the snowball bush, I ran to turn off the ignition so he could hear me gently ask, "How come you get so irritable at times?"

He said the sun had been in his eyes and he hadn't seen me installing the mole trap, then went into this claptrap about why a man's normally benign disposition will sometimes not come up to normal. But this hadn't been one of the times, he assured me.

"Irritability," he said, "can be traced to a couple of characters in our nervous system by the names of Anabolism and Catabolism." Now get this: "These two playmates spend the day serenely teetertottering on a board laid across our cell blocks. At times of frustration, however, the teetering picks up at a pace that causes little Ana, the female, to lose her anchorage, causing Cata, the honcho, to shoot sky-high. The result is irritability." He said for further details, see our family doctor.

Now I ask you, how could anyone in his right mind...but that's another story. The story here is, how could a young girl in her right mind get tied up with such a character in the first place? If you have nothing better to do, like cleaning the oven or taking the laundry to the creek—well, let's begin at the beginning.

In our day, it was every fair maiden's dream to be swept off her roller skates by Errol Flynn looking for a new recruit for his yacht. But when my 16th birthday put me beyond the age limit, I was ripe for the first guy who looked at me twice. (The one I ended up with jokes that he only did so because he couldn't believe it the first time.) And when my mother took the wheels off my roller skates for staying out past the 9:00 curfew one night, I was ready to marry just to get away from home, if

Playing Leapfrog with Porcupines

nothing else. The only alternative was to apply to Ringling Brothers for the job of being shot out of a cannon.

Intuition told me to wear an off white dress to our wedding. My wedding dress was so far off white, it was black. I didn't appreciate how appropriate it was at the time.

You have heard of do-it-yourself individuals? Maynard isn't one of them. He can't even open a box of Wheaties without an owner's manual. You should see him try to get the lid off a tin of sardines. He can't so much as get the key off the bottom without a screwdriver and a pair of pliers. And when it finally drops to the floor and slides under the refrigerator, it's up to me to stop lighting incense, find the key, pick off the cat hairs, and fit the slot in the key over the tab on the tin.

On a good day, he may wind the key all of an inch and a half before the tin strip breaks, runs off the track, or the key refuses to go farther. This leaves me to hunt up my buttonhook. But he's on his own when he begins to hook those physically impaired little stinkers out, body part by body part.

Here's another case in point.

You know those little packets of Wendy's crackers? I've seen kids with stubby fingers open them in nothing flat. Hubby should take lessons from them.

"I don't see why they have to seal these things by thermonuclear fusion," he'll mutter, clawing at the seams. Giving up on this, he tries jabbing an opening with his pen, gnawing on one corner, and (finally) whacking the packet against the edge of the table. Before he can throw the "confounded dumb bunch of crumbs" against the wall, I gently take the packet from him, open it with my bare teeth, and hand it back. He usually forgets to thank me.

The funny thing is (to me, anyway), things that should stay shut, open. (I mean besides his mouth.) For instance, a pair of shoes that close with a single Velcro strap. The strap on the left shoe keeps flopping loose and Velcroing with the right shoe, which causes him to walk like he might be carrying an egg between his knees. And people keep stumbling over one another looking back to see if he actually is carrying an egg between his knees.

My dear husband is also the type who replaces a burned-out light bulb or installs a roll of toilet paper, then struts around as if he's just completed a solo round trip to Mars. Where other towns have their Fix-Up, Paint-Up Weeks, I'm waiting for our little village of Freedom to proclaim a Screw-Up Week, so dear hubby can come into his own.

Selling him on anything involving manual dexterity is like trying to sell Ex-Lax to an American tourist in Mexico. But one day, taking leave of my senses, I suggested that the abandoned upstairs nursery could be converted into a home office for him. What I had in mind, of course, was getting his desk and junk out of the living room so I wouldn't have to keep throwing a sheet over it when we had visitors. To my surprise, that same afternoon, he took the stepladder upstairs, then sawed off one of its legs while using it as a base for haggling off a piece of plywood.

To his credit, before fitting the haggled-off piece around the wall register he had removed the outer flange that held the register in place. But in sawing off the other three legs of the stepladder to even it up, the saw blade had hit the register, sending the core down…down…down the hot air pipe into the bowels of the basement.

Locating the core consumed the remaining time he had allotted for the project. But in tearing the pipe apart (in half a dozen places) searching for the core, we finally found out what had happened to the kids' gerbil that had mysteriously disappeared three years before.

Oh, sure, this man I took to be my lawfully wedded husband has provided a laugh or two among his misadventures during our eon together. I still chuckle over the time he was stapling tile on the kitchen ceiling and stepped barefoot from the stepladder (an aluminum one) onto the range. Funny thing was, one of the burners had been left on. I had never seen a staple gun staple that

Playing Leapfrog with Porcupines

fast—or seen anyone come down off a kitchen range without using a stepladder. Or for that matter, stick his foot in the john.

But getting back to my original story of when he attempted to run me down with his big fat Murray mower and that cockamamie story about Ana and Cata teetering across our cell blocks: If there should be any truth to it, the real reason he might have been out of sorts that day is that he had just come back from a game of golf. Hubby plays in the low 70s; if it gets hotter than that, he prefers to stay in the shade of the 19th hole. But score had nothing to do with little "Ana" losing her anchorage, as he bellyached to me. It was having to play behind a foursome of the "opposing sex."

"I know," he said, "that there are golferesses who can outplay golfers." (That was for my benefit, of course.) "But why must I get behind a foursome whose members haven't seen one another for a month and one has had a baby, one is getting a divorce, one's husband is having an affair, and one has a hearing disability?

"It wasn't so much one of them knocking her ball backwards off the tee on her sixth practice swing. Or hollering 'Look out!' instead of 'Fore!' before beaning a guy putting out on the green ahead. Or spitting on a coin and tossing it into the creek for good luck before hitting the ball into the creek—then taking five minutes to retrieve the ball and ten minutes to locate the blasted coin.

"I'm talking about the one who ran her complete inventory of golf balls through the ball wash and then dried them by sticking a corner of the towel into every lousy dimple. I'm talking about her trying three different areas of real estate before finally locating a spot worthy of her tee—then removing the tee to examine it, I presume, for knotholes. You can't get off a good drive, you know, with wind whistling through a knothole in your tee.

"Then there's the tucking in of the hair, the adjusting of the skirt, the inspecting of the club head to see if it's on securely, the turning of the ball until the 'Trevino' shows, the execution of the perfect back swing for chopping wood, and the stopping at the apex to yell over the shoulder, 'Where's the green?'

"By the time her last worm-burner has dribbled the ball onto it, three of our foursome are dozing on the fairway, and the fourth has seized the opportunity to install new grips on his woods."

From the flecks of foam collecting on hubby's mustache, I guessed that the Bolism kids were a long way from regaining their respective positions on the teetertotter. But luckily, I had not planned on relocating the mole trap; he'd have run me down for sure. I wonder if Ringling is still hiring.

Chapter 11

GONE TO WAIST

More and more of my friends—former friends, actually—have been poking me in the stomach with the comment (and if you've ever been poked in the stomach with a comment, you know the feeling), "Whatever happened to your Greek-god figure?"

And I struggle to keep my Greek-god composure while going into this rather lengthy explanation of how it's my trousers that might be giving the impression that I have recently swallowed a basketball.

How are you fixed for time? I'll be as brief as possible.

The room we added to our rustic abode contains two clothes closets, one for her, one for him. Her closet is along the west wall, his along the north wall. Where they join at the corner, her closet runs across the end of his closet, giving it a full nine feet, while his is thus restricted to a modest 7'6". Even with that disparity, the overflow from her generous closet into his modest closet has caused his off-season wardrobe (as he calls it) to go into the attic with the mice and assorted vermin.

But that's not the half of it. The half of it is what climatic conditions up there are doing to my off-season apparel. Especially my trousers.

Now it's over. I've had it. I am shedding my Mickey Mouse ears and donning Superman's cape. I have turned the other cheek and bared my jugular for the last time. After all, when I took the oath of marriage, it was to have been a 50-50 relationship, not a 9'-7'6". So, cold dinner and a night on the couch or not, I was laying my cards on the table, face up.

That's one reason marriages are breaking up right and left today—lack of communication. It came close in my own family, in fact, before I left home...if you'll excuse my getting personal.

Maynard Good Stoddard

I remember Dad coming home that night and saying to Mother, "Thanks for putting up the scarecrow. I've been meaning to do it."

I remember Mother looking strangely at Dad, not unusual, and saying "I didn't put up the scarecrow."

I remember them going out to investigate and discovering that it was Grandfather. His joints had set while hoeing the rutabagas. Though he recovered nicely, had there been discussion about erecting the scarecrow, Grandfather wouldn't have had to spend most of the afternoon propped up on his hoe.

Back to it:

"It's not so much your usurping closet real estate architecturally designed for the accommodation of my personal raiment," I laid on the table, hoping the sheer power of my vocabulary would quell a smart retort. "But the capricious climate of the attic continues to shrink my stuff until I have become a walking resuscitation case. Even my neckties are shorter."

My dear wife's cheeks still remaining dry, I further pointed out that the waistband on my trousers had downsized to where I haven't had to wear a belt for the past two years. And one of these days a waistband button is going to pop off and put someone's eye out, I said. Adding that lawyers don't defend button-in-the-eye lawsuits for peanuts.

"All I'm asking," I wound up my case, "is my legal half of the closets, where I can hang up at least my off-season pants. Perhaps in time they'll return to normal size and I can again eat a salad without having my circulation cut off."

You know what my dear wife said? Of course you do. Because you have been thinking the very same thing.

Well, both of you—or all three, whatever—are wrong. I have not gone to pot. ("Pot-bellied pig" actually came to mind, now didn't it?) You've heard of the man who wanted to get back to his original weight—7 pounds 4 ounces? I'm not that man. At one time, a flabby and crabby 200, I wanted to melt down to my

Playing Leapfrog with Porcupines

former lean and mean 170. And I did so. And haven't gained ounce one since.

I'll take that back. I did tack on a temporary eight pounds the time I flirted with the Banana Split Diet. I don't mean I followed the Slim Fast regimen of a banana split for breakfast, another for lunch, and then a sensible dinner. Nothing like that. But with the bone-building properties of ice cream, the high fiber in bananas, the pectin from fruit toppings (which must be good for something), combined with the protein found in crushed nuts, I figured the banana split had to be one of the most nutritional of our basic food staples.

After gaining eight pounds, I finally figured out where I had gone wrong. It had to be that lousy maraschino cherry. That's what comes from not reading food labels. Here I had been jeopardizing my Greek-god figure with junk stuff like sodium benzoate, potassium sorbate, sulfur dioxide, and something going by the name "red 40" (which didn't refer to 40 red cherries in the bottle, because I never counted more than 25).

But that eight pounds was soon behind me. Let me rephrase that. (My dear wife says to leave it alone; it's behind me, all right.)

Anyway, continuing her unbroken record for being wrong, she has come up with this crazy theory that sitting at a desk for mmmmm years has caused my chest (why she chuckled here, I don't know) to slide down into my abdominal region. "The attic," she summed up, "has nothing to do with your eyes bulging every time you button your britches."

A retired nurse, she of all people should know better. As patiently as I could, I explained that man has been constructed with a diaphragm for no other purpose than to prevent such a catastrophe. I further pointed out that after years of lugging boulders from the creek bed to create her eight, going on nine, rock gardens, I probably had the strongest diaphragm in Sweet Owen County, if not in the entire state of Indiana. "Including Schwarzenegger's", I said, admittedly getting a tad carried away.

No matter. By this time, dear wife had come up with two strategies for maintaining her illegal footage of closet territory.

One, I could convert an area of the attic into a humidor, she said. Like they keep cigars in. Only bigger, she said. Two, I could store my off-season stuff in the root cellar. At the back, she said. Where it won't interfere with her traffic to the fruit jars, the rutabaga bin, the onion sacks, and the garlic hanging from the rafters, she said.

Number one fell upon deaf ears because clearing the attic for a humidor would mean that most of the junk up there would have to come down and be stored—you know where, and so did I. As for number two, I'd be going to church smelling at best like a highly seasoned pot of Irish stew.

To which dear wife remarked, "It would be an improvement over that bottle of cologne you picked up at the yard sale."

To which I replied...but never mind. With another off-season coming up, I am going to stand on my own hind feet, compress her row of dresses, and hang at least my pants in the reclaimed space, as validated by our 50-50 marital contract.

If they end up in the root cellar, at least I'll have a few pews in church all to myself.

Chapter 12

KICKING THE HABIT—AT AGE 10

What a pity that so many young people today are smoking their lives away and thinking it's the smart thing to do. Especially those budding into adulthood in urban areas. If only they could enjoy the opportunities I took advantage of at the malleable age of ten, they would be kicking the tobacco habit early on—I know that for a fact.

True, I also thought at the time that I might be kicking the bucket as well as the habit—and for a couple of days, I didn't really care which way it went. But what a small price to pay for a long life (*how* long is none of your business) free of those murderous, stinking fumes.

One of the advantages of my young-lion days had to do with living in the quiet little four-corner settlement of Richfield Center, Mich., where a boy's opportunities for flaunting his manhood were somewhat limited. He could chase girls, of course, but upon catching one, it was only to yell, "You're it!"

Or he could give smoking a try.

Here, he had two choices: a "cigarette" constructed from dried corn silk rolled in newspaper, or a charge of ripe burdock seed tamped into a corncob pipe. By coincidence, my memorable, if somewhat brief, smoking career got off the ground via the corn silk and newspaper runway.

On this particular day, I found myself standing in the middle of our sweet corn patch with a page of the *Flint Daily Journal* tucked under my arm. By a stroke of luck, I discovered a supply of kitchen matches in a pocket of my overalls. Selecting a choice hank of corn silk from the nearest stalk, I rolled it neatly in a quarter page of the *Journal*, sealed the seam with saliva, and hunkered down to light up.

At the postmortem, veteran corn silkers concluded that most likely I had failed to generate enough saliva sufficient to seal a

Maynard Good Stoddard

quarter page. They further agreed that a one-eighth pager would not have caused the flareup that had reduced my eyebrows to pipestem cleaners. I didn't mention that dropping the conflagration into my lap hadn't been my finest five seconds, either.

Not until the next day did my taste buds resume their proper function and my voice return to its normal, dulcet, soprano pitch. It required less time than that, however, for dear old Dad, a former boy himself, to interpret the cause of my eyebrow clinkers. By way of acknowledgment, he allowed me the honor of leading the way to the woodshed.

Anyone with even half the brains of a goose would have retired from the smoking game right here, of course. But not me. Oh, no. I had to open my flat little ears to the contentions of my peers that for pure smoking pleasure, burdock seed in a corncob pipe was the only way to go.

So what did you do, Maynard? I'll tell you what I did. Under the pretext of a yen for blowing bubbles—which would have been a better (much better) idea—I shot a week's allowance for this five-cent corncob pipe and headed directly for the haymow to look for ripe seed from the burdock, of the genus *Arctium*, meaning "arcs when heated."

Corn silk and burdock seed turned out to be pretty much on a par when it came to taste bud nullifying, cough inducing, and eye watering. But where corn silk had a tendency to bald the brow and torch the trousers, hot burdock seed tended to pop out of the pipe and land on the nose. Dear old Dad had to take only one look at those potholes in my honker, of course, and it was back to ye olde woodshed, my home away from home.

And that did it, right? No, not yet. Although I am belatedly giving Dad credit for having a hand in my swearing off the evil weed for good, that hand was not above taking the wrinkles out of the seat of my pants on a regular basis.

My dad, you see, owned the lone grocery store occupying one of the four corners at Richfield Center. And on the men's side of the store, he had this glass-enclosed tobacco case, which

Playing Leapfrog with Porcupines

he kept right out there in plain sight on the counter. It was there he had introduced a box of the cutest little store-bought cigars that ever a budding manhood-flaunter had ever feasted his bloodshot eyes on.

Just between us—now that the statute of limitations has expired by some 70 years—the cute little "Between-the-Acts" cigar that came into my possession was not store-bought; I swiped it. My dad owning the store, as I said, and this beauty being no larger than a cigarette, my crime had to be the pettiest of all petty thefts. Nevertheless, I felt it to be in the best interest of my backside to wait until the sole customer had his back turned and my pappy was probing in the pickle barrel before helping myself to one of those tantalizing, miniature sticks of dynamite going under the alias of "cigar" and heading for the flour and feed building behind the store.

I remember sitting down on a sack of oats. I remember thinking this would be my first smoke without apprehension for reducing my eyebrows to nubbins, kindling my corduroys, or dimpling my snout. The rest is hearsay.

And what I heard say was, my brother, Meryl, and another potential pallbearer, Ronald Seeley, by a stroke of luck stumbled upon my corpse before it had time to cool. Upon a convenient green window shutter, they arranged my remains and bore them home to Mother.

My complexion and the shutter by this time being of the same hue, Mother, having never been a boy herself, diagnosed my condition as a severe case of collywobbles. Not so with dear old Dad, who had no trouble putting his finger on the cause of my affliction. By a second stroke of fortune, however, my inability to walk precluded another trip to you-know-where and the laying on of his hand to you-know-what.

I haven't looked tobacco in the face since. I'll take that back. Along about age 30, attempting to enhance my image as a writer, I bought a genuine meerschaum and a can of "Velvet" tobacco—another misnomer of the nicotine industry. Not that it mattered a whole lot. I had no sooner got the members glowing nicely on the initial test run than I bit down on the pipe stem, breaking off a front tooth and spreading the glowing embers liberally across my nose. *That* was the last time I looked tobacco in the face.

The bottom line is, I haven't spent a small fortune over the years catering to an incorrigible smoking habit. I don't have cancer. I don't suffer the irreparable gasps of emphysema. I've been spared the enormous expense of a lung transplant and the complete wipeout of heart bypass surgery. My family's health has not been jeopardized by their having to breathe years of passive smoke.

In other words, even if I had paid for that deceptive little Between-the Acts seducer, it would have been the best investment I ever made.

Chapter 13

INVEST NOT THY WHOLE WAD

Before you begin thawing out some of your frozen assets to transplant in the speculative soil of Wall Street, I'd like a few words (exactly 1,337, as it turns out) with you.

You may be confused (I know I was) by divergent sayings emanating from the Street. One saying warns "Invest not they whole wad." Another one says, "The only way to come out of the market with a small fortune is to go into the market with a large fortune."

As you should already know (otherwise, this is no place for you), participants in the market are divided into two camps: the Bulls (optimists) and the Bears (pessimists). I was neither. I started out as a Hog and came out a Chicken. Having neither a whole wad nor a large fortune, I wondered what would happen if I went into the market with only half a wad. The answer is, I came out with my shirt. And I was lucky to have that.

But don't go away. In the process of watching my dollars dwindle to this 50 percent polyester, 50 percent cotton, size M, I stumbled upon an investment strategy that has turned April 15 into one of the happiest days of the year. And before you turn your wad over to the Wall Street wolves, I suggest you listen up.

With dreams of yachts, spas, limos, eyeglasses with stained-glass lenses, and monogrammed toothpicks dancing in my head, I began my invasion of Wall Street by buying 100 shares of Thortec at $20^{3/8}$ (dollars, that is) per share. When the stock promptly dropped to a bargain at $17^{1/2}$, I shrewdly added another hundred. By the time it had descended to three, my portfolio boasted a neat 1,000 shares, primed and ready to take off like a goosed gazelle.

At 9/16—or $56^{1/4}$ cents—I cleverly executed what is known as the "bigger fool" strategy by dumping the whole load on a poor novice in the market. It's a dog-eat-dog, you know.

"So, how much did you lose?" will, of course, be your first question. As it was my dear wife's first question. But, as I pointed out to her, there's this saying: "There is no gain except by loss." (You could look it up.) When something in the glaze that formed over her eyes told me that she wasn't quite clear on this point, I took her—as I'm now taking you—to Tax Form 1040, Schedule D, Capital Gains and Losses, Line 20: "If line 19 is a loss, enter it as a loss on Form 1040, line 13."

"With this loss," I said, "our taxes this year will be cut to a nubbin." But why is it that a woman who can decipher the hieroglyphics of crocheting directions can't understand a simple principle of economics?

Nevertheless, once I had caught onto this strategy, there was no stopping me. By avoiding the pitfalls of comparing a company's current assets to liabilities, working out its price-earnings ratio, checking its long-term debt, earnings record, and management background, I took on 600 shares of Pennsylvania Engineering. When it, in remarkably short order, folded its tent, I quietly stole away with another neat tax loss of $1,200.

You may resent my continuing to boast like this, but I can't help mentioning how I snapped up 200 shares of Arrow Electronics at $19^{1/2}$, adding another 100 shares at $14^{1/4}$. Sold the first 200 at five, the 100 at $5^{1/2}$. And barely in time. At this writing, the stock has hit $35^{3/8}$. I still get chills thinking of the tax if I'd hung onto that baby.

Oracle Systems would bring me even closer to a disaster. I bought 200 shares of that dude in January at $8^{1/8}$. Couldn't figure out why this stock would tread water for six entire months. The answer turned out to be me. Once I gave up on it, Oracle Systems headed due north, arriving at a price of 64 only a year later. The stock has since split two for one and headed now for who-knows-where. I'm still sweating over that one.

Timing, as you can see, must be credited with much of my success. Knowing when to hold 'em and when to fold 'em. Even street-smart veterans will hang onto a stock like the proverbial puppy to a root, even while it continues to go up, up, up, finally

Playing Leapfrog with Porcupines

getting out right at the very top. They don't seem to realize what they're in for.

But, thanks to stocks like Crime Control, College Life, Alphanumeric, Solar Equinox, and I don't know how many others (my dear wife could tell you, but I have lost count), I have learned that there'll come a day when the company's CEO will come down with a head cold, or quarterly earnings will plunge by one cent a share, and the stock will drop like a rock. Then a stockholder can get out without having that big tax axe hanging over his head.

One question I am often asked (most often by dear wife) is, "How do you come up with these rocks that offer so much tax relief?"

I would like to credit my own sagacity, of course. But, to be truthful (strange as that word may sound, coming from me), I must include several sources for my tax-loss triumphs.

A "stockbroker" has been so named because a client who responds to his tips most often ends up broker than when relying on his own stock selections. For one of my numerous examples, I refer to College Life. The broker talked me into 100 shares at $10^{1/2}$. It went directly to 21. Talk about your sleepless nights! But not to worry.

When the stock finally "dipped" to $17^{1/2}$, I took the broker's advice to snap up another 100 shares. (Which reminds me, I never did thank him.) From $17^{1/2}$, College Life continued to dip until the stock certificates finally joined those of Pennsylvania Engineering and the others now decorating the west wall of my home office. With a lacelike border in light purple, they are really lovely.

Nor must I forget the sage advice of the "stock analyst," an animal to be found in publications such as *The Wall Street Journal, Barron's,* and *Forbes,* as well as "Wall Street Week" and "The Nightly Business Report" on the tube. The more laudatory the praise, the more assurance I have that the analyst has been caught with the stock and is trying to unload it on the "bigger fool." Had I not adopted this bigger fool role in several instances, I'm sure I wouldn't be enjoying the tax status I hold today.

Finally, I pay careful attention to the letter dreamed up by the president to his stockholders in the annual report. Whenever I read of the "one-time adversities" that have temporarily brought the company to its knees, and the surefire convalescent strategy for the year ahead, I know I've got a sure tax-loss tiger by the tail.

The one catch to my modus operandi: the IRS allows but a $3,000 capital loss per year; the remainder must be carried over. As I have tried to explain to my dear wife, I am staying in the market primarily to build up this carry-over to where it will last for as many years as she does. I'm not sure she fully understands.

As this carry-over may well be all that I will be leaving her, I've warned her not to go messing with the AT&Ts, the Chryslers, the Oracle Systems, and that bunch. Otherwise, all the work I'm doing now could go down the drain in a hurry.

If she—and you—have been paying attention, I want to wish you all a very happy April 15, this year and for years to come.

Chapter 14

...AND NOTHING BUT

"Why don't you enter the liar's contest this year?" my dear wife said to me, having just finishing proofreading my latest brilliant literary effort. "I believe it's held somewhere in Wisconsin."

"Whatever for?" I asked, batting my big brown innocent eyes. "I may occasionally take a few liberties with the truth, but I'm certainly not what you could call an out-and-out liar."

"No? How about your aunt who contracted tuberculosis from licking Christmas seals? Or that other aunt—Prunella, wasn't it?—walking home from Wednesday night prayer meeting who was run down by a rusty police car and died of lockjaw? All true, I suppose."

"You've heard of hearsay? That's what I heard say."

"And I suppose it was hearsay that one of your nephews drowned in a watermelon-eating contest?"

"Correct."

"How about the uncle during the Great Depression who had to take a job sitting behind the front window of an Italian restaurant eating spaghetti and meatballs from 10:00 a.m. to 5:00 p.m.—with an hour off for lunch?"

"I think you made that up."

"I can look it up, if I have to. As for your grandfather breaking his leg falling over the pattern in your living room carpet..."

"The next time I buy shirts, remind me to get a larger collar."

"Then there was that trash about everyone at our wedding throwing rice except for my mother, who threw a tomato. Practically ruined your new brand new sweatshirt."

"Okay, so she missed. But it was close."

"And your dog that treed a moose."

"I didn't say he treed a moose. I said he barked *as if* he'd treed a moose. You can look that up, too."

"How about the stuff of your digging a trench to drain the basement into the pond and, instead, you drained the pond into the basement."

"I never did get credit for at least trying."

"You know what I think? I think you've got a hole in your ozone layer. Your parents giving you a pet lamb that was allergic to wool—of all things!"

"Itchabod, I called him. Never could catch the little feller."

"I suppose that included in your hearsays is that crud about your cousin."

"What crud about what cousin?"

"The crud about the cousin twice removed—removed once to Leavenworth, the second time to Sing Sing. The one released from Sing Sing a few days before Christmas who stopped off in New York City to pick up a few gifts for the folks back home. The one who fractured three vertebrae and ruptured his spleen falling down a flight of hotel stairs with an armload of Gideon Bibles."

"Oh, *that* cousin."

"And how about that cousin's twin brother?"

"I didn't know he had a brother."

"Probably didn't. But that couldn't stop you from shooting off your big fat typewriter about what a hog-wild deer hunter he was. How he finally bought a house on 40 acres in northern Michigan—where deer played on his lawn through the summer, ate up his garden, and rubbed against the posts on his front porch until the posts finally fell.

"Come opening day of the hunting season, as you likely heard say, he strolled out after breakfast to bag the biggest buck, only to find nothing but fence-to-fence deer hunters. Not a deer in sight."

"I vaguely recall hearing that,"

"And do you recall that after not sighting a deer the entire two weeks, on the evening before the deadline, he went into

Playing Leapfrog with Porcupines

town, bought a set of deer antlers and a deer call, and stopped at a neighbor's to borrow a moth motel that at one time had served as a raccoon coat?"

"That's possible."

"But here the crud thickens.

"According to your vague recollection, early the final morning found him back on his favorite runway, where he strapped the antlers to his head, ran the barrel of his rifle down a sleeve of the raccoon coat, squatted down beside a stump, and then began blowing on the deer call.

"At the funeral, perhaps you'll recall, you first met your aunt Flossie who was sitting in a wheelchair, her hair frizzled white from having inadvertently turned on her electric blanket while eating watermelon in bed. Or so you were told, I suppose."

"I must have been told that, of course. I certainly wouldn't have made it up."

"Can you say that about the pumpkins you were raising on a milk diet, and the vines went across the fence and milked your neighbor's cows dry? Or the glass eye you found in the tapioca?"

"I'm always the one who gets the pit in the cherry pie and the pebble in the baked beans. You know that."

"And the hole in the ozone layer. Getting your head caught between the boards while nailing up the board fence! Really! And knocking your seatmate across the airplane aisle while trying to open your packet of peanuts! And your nearsighted golfing partner who came into the club dance wearing a divot in place of his toupee. I just don't know."

"It was getting dark and he had swung so hard heading into the final hole that his rug had come off. I believe I cleared that up satisfactorily."

"You didn't even try to clear up that stuff about your door-to-door selling. How the woman ran out to hold her charging wolfhound and her little kid bit you in the leg."

"I carried that scar for years."

"You've also carried all that nonsense about what your Aunt Flossie expounded on while you were waiting for the serviceman to come and change the flat tire on the hearse."

"On the contrary, I don't remember that at all."

"According to her, according to you, your Uncle Quonse was the only one in your entire lineage to experience even a trace of good luck.

"His full name, you may vaguely bring to mind was Quonset, after the Quonset hut, the long, low building erected as a temporary shelter during World War II. Uncle Quonse's head had the same long, low shape. As you supposedly were told, two weeks before he was born, his mother had run into a mailbox. Prenatal influence, someone else had pointed out."

"I don't remember exactly who that was...Are you sure you didn't shrink this shirt the last time you laundered it?"

"It hasn't been laundered. That's the shirt you got on sale as a Slight Irregular. All I did was cut off the third sleeve.

"As for the rest of your hoopla about Uncle Quonse: Unable to scratch out a living on his acreage of rocks and clay, he had taken a job as punch press operator at the South Fisher Body Plant in nearby Flint. Three days is all it took for him to routinely trip the press before removing his finger, and the press had accommodatingly removed it for him. A second surprise came in the form of an insurance check for the handsome sum of $500. He had immediately quit and gone back to farming. Do these exact words stir your memory buds?"

"This shirt collar is killing me."

"Droning right along, when Uncle Quonse saw how well that insurance thing worked out, he immediately took out a policy sponsored by *The Flint Daily Journal*. For 25 cents a week, it covered all accidents on the farm. Again I quote, 'The very day that policy went into effect, darned if Uncle Quonse didn't back over his wife with the manure spreader.'"

"I'm sure I would never put anything like that in print."

"You can't deny saying that even *his* luck ran out eventually. You claim Uncle Quonse got religion, as you used to say in

Playing Leapfrog with Porcupines

Michigan, and he was drowned in the Flint River while being baptized."

"It's possible."

"You're out of your gourd."

"How about if the preacher said he couldn't be baptized with his hat on? And Uncle Quonse telling him he wasn't going to take it off? And the preacher saying yes, he was? And Uncle Quonse replying, 'Not in that cold water'? And the preacher saying he'd see about that? And in the struggle, Uncle Quonse stepping out too far and the current taking him?"

"And are you still of the opinion that the baptism was a success, because the preacher managed to save Uncle Quonse's hat?"

"I'll give it more thought on my way to Wal-Mart. I've got to get some $16^{1/2}$-inch collars. I can hardly breathe in this thing."

Chapter 15

BORROWING TROUBLE

As I emerged from another long day's lonesome hibernation in my den of dreams, my dear wife looked up from her task of clipping grocery coupons and said, "Barnyard [her pet name for me], if you ever had to go to work, what would you want to do?"

Counting to ten, and then ten more, I put the insinuation on hold and began thinking (something I rarely do after 5:00 p.m.). What *would* I do if I didn't go into my playroom every morning (but Sunday) and amuse myself with my capricious pen, my patient legal pad, my hide-and-seek games with dictionary and thesaurus, and those friendly frolics with typewriter and fax?

"I suppose you'd laugh if I said I've often thought that photographing lingerie models would be a pleasant way of making a living." She laughed.

"You can't hold a camera still when you're photographing the dog," she said, wiping the tears from her eyes.

"I could always serve as a handyman, don't forget. Kick that around in your empty stadium."

"Handyman!" I thought she would have a convulsion. "After some of the dumb stuff you have pulled?"

"Such as?" I could have bitten my tongue to the quick.

"Such as painting our garage at Whitmore Lake, for starters."

So she had begun this discourse to bring up the old Whitmore Lake garage episode for the 37th time. But as I again pointed out, this disaster came from a rented paint sprayer, not from incompetence on my part.

I know. Shakespeare tells us neither a borrower nor a renter be. (Or is it lender? Whatever.) I had learned the value of this admonition waaay back when I was young and gay (make that young and free). If it was starters my dear wife wanted, I'd give

Playing Leapfrog with Porcupines

her a starter she hadn't known about: it goes back to the night I borrowed my brother Meryl's 100 percent soybean suit.

For this catastrophe I blame Henry Ford. Had he stuck to turning out his Model A's and not begun fooling around with various uses for this hog staple, the suit would not have darkened a hanger in our dark upstairs closet.

Basic black with a quarter-inch green vertical stripe, the suit could be seen coming from 50 feet away on a foggy night. This asset alone was reason enough for brother Meryl to lay out the handsome sum of $18 to remove it from the rack at the cut-rate haberdashery in downtown Flint.

I "borrowed" the suit to wear to the big Saturday night dance held weekly in Russelville. My explanation to Meryl that I had mistaken the suit for one of mine didn't hold water, because the thing actually glowed in the dark, and neither of mine did. What did hold water, unfortunately, was the suit.

No sooner had I picked up my date for this particular bash than rain began to fall in great gobs. Though I had no trouble delivering her nice and dry at the dance hall entrance, I did have trouble finding a parking place for our Model A. Thus, by the time I arrived back under shelter, the proverbial drowned rat and I had much in common. And brother Meryl's basic black soybean suit with the seductive green stripe had assumed the pungent odor that rises from beans that farmers cook in a big iron kettle out behind the barn to allow the stench to dissolve before it can penetrate the house.

As a result, no sooner had I grappled with my date for our first dance than she straight-armed me, keeping me at arm's length until we arrived at the LADIES ROOM sign, where she excused herself. When she emerged, it was only to explain that she wasn't feeling well and, by the way, she had made other arrangements for getting home.

The odor hung, close to visibility, in the old family sedan for a full month. And when I left home for college, the 100 percent soybean suit was still hanging from a nail in the woodshed.

But if my dear wife preferred the Whitmore Lake garage episode for starters, the garage it would be.

"Why didn't you paint the garage with your trusty old three-inch brush, instead of renting an unreliable sprayer?" I have often been asked. By the same person each time. To which my response has been, "Because after its last use, the bristles swore an oath never to be separated again." If she wanted to use the brush for tenderizing Swiss steak, it was all hers. But I wasn't going to slap on three gallons of paint with a brush that would have required at least a week for the bristles to be separated into singles.

Why three gallons, for Pete's sake? The blame here can be traced directly to the army surplus people. When I spot an ad for outside gray paint at two bucks per gallon, three for five, well, you know me.

So I hie down to the Whitmore Lake hardware, rent this humongous paint sprayer, and fill it with light gray army surplus. Then, accompanied by Nikki, still trusting her dad by age four, and Tippie, our equally innocent cocker, I lead the way out to our target.

Holding the sprayer at eye level, no small trick in itself, I took aim from a distance of maybe four feet and pulled the trigger. Rather than the fine mist I had expected, a stream rivaling the circumference of a ballpoint pen shot out, bounced off the siding, and surplused my daughter and my dog from head to toe and head to tail, respectively. Although they both cleaned up pretty well, I still have some of that gray in my hair to this very day.

"And don't forget how you butchered our house in Indianapolis with the floor sander," dear wife busted in.

How come a woman can dredge up a minor boo-boo from that long ago and not remember how expertly I did something only last week? Like...well...let's see...h'm...

The sander business had less to do with my lack of ability, as I keep reminding her, than with the terms of the rental

Playing Leapfrog with Porcupines

agreement: half a day for half the cost of a full day. And you know me, as I may have already mentioned.

Professional sanding people will be asking, I'm sure, how I could sand the floors of three bedrooms, the dining room, and a hallway in just short of four hours. No problem really. One secret is to use only course sandpaper, forget the fine. Another little trick is to go cross grain instead of with the grain. By doing so, you can really make the old wood chips fly and get the sander returned before the noon deadline.

Had dear wife not got into the act and varnished the floors, we might have remained on speaking terms for the rest of that month. Why varnish would bring out the hollows, the pits, the potholes, and various other irregularities has never been cleared up in any varnish books I have read. A know-it-all relative, who turned an ankle in one of the valleys, pointed out that I should have gone with the grain and that the sander should have been elevated at the end of each "furrow," as he nastily phrased it. But after pointing out to him that I had sanded four rooms and a hallway in less than four hours, he just sat there with his mouth open, but nothing came out. Dear wife, on the other hand, still talks about it, given the slightest opportunity.

Nor does she fail to point out that borrowing or renting isn't necessary. She says I can cause trouble enough using our own stuff, the snow blower being her favorite.

I blame the medical people for this catastrophe. I wouldn't have bought the blasted blower had I not read that men my age who shoveled snow were dropping like flies. I would like to ask the clown who came up with this longevity tidbit what's the difference between keeling over from shoveling snow and going to your reward from trying to start and operate a mulish, clattering, smoking, no-good piece of junk. But I'm getting ahead of myself.

You don't pour just plain old gasoline into a snow blower. You must carefully follow the recipe for mixing in the proper amount of oil or risk, I suppose, the embarrassment of blowing out all eight cylinders. After squeezing a Primer Bulb to send this mixture from tank to carburetor, you must remember to turn the key to ON. (Extremely important, as I would discover after try number ten on the Rewind Manual Starter, without so much as an encouraging belch.) It was my dear wife who discovered the Choke. But not until she had read in the manual that "the Control Bar must be engaged at all times" did the blower at last begin chewing up the plywood flooring of our shed.

I take you now—along with the remains of the snow blower—to place of purchase. A no-receipt-no-refund type of individual emerged from behind the counter, lifted a loose panel of the blower with the toe of his Florsheims, and coolly asked, "You been throwing stones at this poor thing?"

"We have a stone driveway," I explained.

"Our snow blowers are made to operate on concrete," he frostily informed me.

"Our only concrete is in the root cellar," I icily pointed out. "And we don't get much snow down there."

Why I left the wreckage to be repaired (at $135) has never been cleared up satisfactorily to you-know-who. Her main beef comes from my not having used the snow blower since.

On our way home from place of purchase, we spotted a car with a flat tire, and the driver just stood there staring at it. Whether he was swearing or praying for help, I couldn't detect. But big-hearted old me had to stop to find out.

He needed a jack. And I had a jack, a brand-new $40 Wal-Mart hydraulic jack, never used. I would be glad to see him use it so I could pass the knowledge along to dear wife, as I am often too exhausted from driving under her tutelage to take on any extracurricular activities.

It so happened that I had no more than returned to our car to pass along the knowledge than the man took off, jack and all.

And I didn't have a spare 40 bucks at that time to buy a new one.

I thought of borrowing a jack, of course...but only briefly.

Chapter 16

MUM'S THE WORD

The other evening, while listening to my favorite music ("Opus to a Field Mouse" by Rinseyourcorsetoff), my dear wife emerged from the kitchen with her lips moving.

Turning off the opus, I walked over and asked if she had said something. It turned out she had announced a surprise dinner ready on the table. The surprise, as far as I could tell, lay in the fact that she had prepared a meal without the smoke alarm going off. But perhaps I had been concentrating more on the problem we were having with communications.

I am not suggesting that the Creator made a mistake in creating the human body, so please don't quote me. I'm just saying that it would be nice if earflaps on the human body would continue to grow as we advance in years. Not until they hang down on our shoulders, or anything like that, but enough so that we could continue to hear people who don't speak up.

You may also have noticed how more people are muttering, instead of enunciating clearly. I don't have to leave our house to notice this.

My dear wife contends that I am the cause of her having to reply to my witticisms with a "What?" "Hmm?" "Come again?" or—should we be infested with company at the time—"I'm sorry, honcho honey, but I didn't catch that."

Getting her to do something about her hearing problem is like getting my new dog to climb the flagpole. (He's not the quick study Brutus was. Brutus could climb that flagpole before he could talk, as I remember.) Dear wife argues that her hearing is OK; it's my speaking in lowercase that is causing the trouble.

I tell her that if my words are not understandable, it's not a matter of volume; it's because the only way I can get them in is edgewise. This usually ends our communicating for the day. No loss without a little gain, as the saying goes.

Maynard Good Stoddard

The strange thing is, although five years her elder, I can hear as well as I ever did—that is, except when she goes into her mumbling mode. And if I ask her what it was she mumbled, I often regret that I didn't bite my tongue instead.

Only last night, by holding both earflaps straight out and watching her lips, did I finally interpret her mumbling to be, "Rather than having me make a clown suit for that costume party why don't you just stick a couple of straws up your nose and go as a walrus?"

She thought she'd made a joke. But like most veteran wives she doesn't realize that married men have feelings, just like the more fortunate.

It's not only my dear wife. Talking in undertones seems to be "going around" like the flu bug. Movie actors, TV sitcom-ers, friends, former friends—all have caught it. But if the screen and the tube people think lower voices are more dramatic, I have news for them. I've strained my ear muscles for the last time trying to catch a phrase here and there. The only movies I watch now are the ones with Schwarzenegger and the "Home Alones." Machine guns and pratfalls require no interpretation.

Talk shows evidently present the same problem—not that I am a fan. However, the other day while trying to flip the remote to an exercise program on PBS, I happened across one of those shows, the theme of which (as nearly as I could tell) had to do with how these female guests had forfeited their maidenhoods.

In my haste to switch channels, I inadvertently hit the volume button. And even with the windows rattling, it was all I could do to make out that this one girl had kissed her maidenhood good-bye on the Ferris wheel at Six Flags.

I'll tell you the truth (strange as that may sound), if it were not for nature shows and "The Nightly Business Report," I would sell our three TV sets and buy a hearing aid for my dear wife. Getting her to use it would be another matter, of course. (I married a proud woman—but a real lady, I hasten to add. She always goes to the curb to spit.)

Playing Leapfrog with Porcupines

Since this voice fallout fad began, I have been turning from the wasteland of television to literature's rich loam. But what is happening here shouldn't be happening to—well, to me, that's who (or *whom,* for you prudish).

I'm referring to the way our industrial giants are now competing to see which giant can wring the most lard out of its operation. I'm especially referring to the publishers of books, magazines, newspapers, lawn mower manuals, medicine bottle labels, cereal box ingredients, and other printed matters.

Printers used to ink their rollers from gallon jugs, but since this economy kick, they must be applying the ink from shot glasses. The way I look at it (which is dimly), these printing giants could find ways of staying out of the red other than by taking the black out of their printing. It has gotten so bad that sometimes I am required to use a magnifying glass on the papers and news magazines to see who did what to whom.

Another giant that has been shrunk to midget size involves our telephone company. I realize that competition is tough, but surely there must be a more humane way of saving bucks than by reducing the circumference of phone lines to the point that a call from a neighbor sounds as though it's coming from across the Atlantic on a frayed cable.

I refer you to a call made only last week. Timed, as usual, to get me up from the dinner table (for which I should have been thankful, I suppose, as we were having recycled succotash), the caller turned out to be a friendly fellow, knew me by my first name, and wanted to know how I was feeling. He even asked—if I understood him right—if we owned our own home. What this had to do with my "writing," I couldn't figure out. However, thinking that he surely must be complimenting me, I kept answering "I appreciate it," "Thank you very much," You're very kind," things like that.

The next day, a truck came up the drive groaning under a load of aluminum siding. Not until I had proved to the driver and his two helpers that, thanks to the termites, the framework of our house could no longer support aluminum siding did they let me off the hook.

I've suffered even greater embarrassments from the muffled mouthings of my friends—former friends, to be precise. Instead of asking these undertoners to repeat, I began answering, "I agree," You can say that again," "You're absolutely right," and "Right on." But no more—not since I replied to one good buddy, "I know that for a fact." What my once good buddy had confided to me was, "I think my wife is cheating on me."

That was the "coop de grass," as Jimmy Durante once mangled the phrase. No more trying to cover up for these people with the soft palates. Until this fad runs its course, I'll be cupping my ear and asking them right out, "What?" "Hmm?" "How's that?" or "Come again?" This will at least let them know that what they are trying to communicate is not going in one ear, much less coming out the other.

To spare my dear wife the hassle of cupping and "hmming," I have begun speaking a couple of decibels above my normal dulcet voice, to which she has begun to respond, "YOU DON'T HAVE TO SHOUT!" I may begin writing notes and leaving them on the refrigerator. Other suggestions would be appreciated.

Chapter 17

ANTS ARE NO PICNIC

Since the first picnic off the Ark, the ant has been touted as the smartest, most sociable, and hardest working nuisance in all insectdom. Even King Solomon, sharp as he was, advised us to "Go to the ant, thou sluggard; to observe her ways, and be wise."

Now along comes an entomologist from the University of California who knocks this proverb in the head by stating, "Science has finally caught up with the ants. They are lazy, not busy, industrious workers. Individual ants spend a great deal of time just loafing."

Well, I am not a sluggard, in spite of what you might hear if you were to tap our phone. But having believed in Solomon since reading how he settled the squabble of two mothers over ownership of a baby by ordering it cut in two and giving each mother half, my curiosity was piqued. If the entomologist was right, then King Solomon didn't know his ants from a hole in the ground. I had to find out.

If you are an ant lover, maybe you'd better sit down for this...

The ant, gentle reader, is not only a sluggard herself (Solomon's choice of gender, certainly not mine) she is also stupid, wasteful, obstinate, and sadistic. As for morals...well!

That the ant is a shirker is easily proved. All you have to do is catch one, paint its gaster (or rear end if you prefer) a fluorescent pink for easy identification, then turn the little four-flusher loose. You thought ants were working their little gasters off when racing around in high gear, right? Well, keep your eye on this one with the pink caboose. It will zip past you a dozen times in less than a minute without the foggiest notion of where it's going or what it's supposed to be doing. Except, that is, for giving the appearance of being busy, in case King Solomon should still be around.

Or talk about dumb! Blindfold one of these mini-charlatans (or put it in a matchbox if you aren't that good at blindfolding an ant) and drop the dummy no more than five feet from its diggings. Theory has it that the ant will cleverly use "polarization of light" to find its way back. But what happens? The panic-stricken fraud will take off, like a wild horse, in all directions, without once bothering to polarize the light. It's obvious that uppermost in its miniscule mind is how come the colony moved without leaving at least a forwarding address.

I once spotted one of these fakers standing tiptoe on the very tip of my car antenna. Looking for the nearest picnic? Contemplating suicide? Considering a bungee jump? No, simply proving that when it came to directions, it didn't know its gaster from its elbow.

In all fairness, more intense research than mine shows certain ants to be respectable harvesters, herders, soldiers, sentries, nursemaids, janitors, and foragers. But for every respectable ant, research also has turned up lowlifes such as masters with slaves, beggars, robbers, permanent guests, parasites, kidnappers, and yes, murderers.

The thief ant exercises its Solomonic wisdom by establishing a colony next door to larger ants for the sole purpose of pilfering their food. The larger ants can't chase the dirty little crooks because they have made the passageway too small. Although the larger ants are born excavators, it doesn't occur to the simpletons to enlarge the tunnel and retrieve their stolen property.

Another phenomenon of questionable intelligence has been observed by a respected professor of ant lore. "Most pheromones (chemical substances) are specific," he reports, "carrying just one message. A dead ant, for example, emits a pheromone that signals other ants to dispose of the body. When daubed on an ant that's alive, the pheromone still compels the ant's mates to dutifully dump it on their trash heap outside the nest. It may resist ("Hey, come on, you guys, this ain't funny!") and scramble back home, but until the pheromone evaporates it'll be carted back again and again to the burial heap."

Or consider the subgenus *Colobpis* tribe, who live within plant materials. This rabble has soldiers whose heads resemble closely in texture and color the exterior of the nest. Their job is to act like a cork in a bottle. On duty, the soldier stands with its head in the doorway, which has been carved to conform in size and shape to the soldier's head. When an ant returns to the nest, it touches the "head door" with its antennae. The soldier backs up, allows the ant to enter, then resumes its position. Not the most thrilling of occupations, but so far so good.

The blueprint falls off the drawing board, however, whenever the soldier belongs to the *Cryptocerus texanus* gang, feared as the roughest, most sadistic outfit west of the Pecos. Instead of backing up, it has this mean habit of only crouching in position, making the entering ant crawl over. For amusement, the bored soldier loves to end the crouch before the incomer has cleared. This causes the victim to be squeezed between the doorkeeper and the roof of the passageway. It can holler "uncle" till it's blue in the face, but it stays pinned until the soldier resumes a crouch for the next caller. And the sooner the better, we are left to conjecture.

Unless you observe these pretenders closely (and this is where Solomon might have screwed up), ants appear to be working in harmony. If they're building a nest, "Here, let me help you with that roof beam, Sarah," is what they would like you to think. But the truth is, each ant is doing it's own thing, to heck with Sarah. If the dirt she throws out of the kitchen happens to land in the bedroom, tough.

Transporting prey, ants will not put their minds, so called, to the problem but will work out the situation by trying various expedients. "Okay now, you go that way and we'll go this way…no, we'll go that way and you guys back up…all right, you turn around and…" and in doing so they drop their end, and right on top of poor Bertha who has been looking for another expedient.

But that's not the whole tragedy. A pair of *Formica lugubris* workers produce about 8.0×10^{-6} horsepower as compared with

3.2×10^{-6} for single ants (and those formulas aren't as easy to work out as you might think). Only about 75 percent of that horsepower is used, however; the rest being wasted in opposing the efforts of the other ant. So when you see a dozen of these little filchers struggling to sneak a deviled egg from your picnic table, half the bunch are dragging their feet and the half bearing the brunt of the load are falling over them. This may be pure speculation, but if you were to put a magnifying glass over the ones bearing the brunt, what you'd likely find is at least four of the six with hernias.

Ants have a reputation for being sociable, right? Through a magnifying glass I watched a couple of ants "socializing" on our patio only this week. Were they sipping aphid milk while swapping lies about stretch marks from their honeypot days? No. One bosom buddy had sunk her teeth into the leg of her companion and wouldn't let go. I watched this tableau of fellowship for a full 30 minutes before the bitee finally relinquished her leg to the biter, and hobbled off.

An isolated incident? Not according to an entomologist with more ant-hours than mine. He reports that once an ant has clamped its mandibles (jaws, if you prefer) onto something, they remain clamped even after its head has been severed. Survivors of a battle between two colonies can often be seen, he says, with several heads fastened to their legs. Call it the virtue of stick-to-itivenes, if you like. I go along with Kipling that "if you can keep your head when all others about you are losing theirs, you're a smarter ant than I am, Gunga Din," or however that goes.

The fire ant is another species that projects the image of its genre as a faithful, hardworking defender of its colony, flag, and constitution. In case you have never consorted with this group— as I did recently while pulling weeds from our daughter's patio in South Carolina—a fire ant is to the skin what jalapeno peppers are to the palate. All I got from observing the ways of these diminutive blowtorches were arms that burned and itched for the next two days. I carried the red spots for a week.

Playing Leapfrog with Porcupines

As for the ant's more intimate habits, I am not one to pass judgment. I can only report that the brief but glamorous nuptial is orchestrated by the queen of the colony, who has wings, taking off and flying higher and higher until but a lone suitor (males also have wings) is her only pursuer. How this evidence was obtained, don't ask. I have it on good authority that the moment the marriage is consummated, her wings fall off and he drops dead.

Go the ants? No, thank you, I've been to the ants, I have observed their ways. And you can have them.

Chapter 18

THINGS THAT GO BUMP IN THE DAYTIME

I'm sitting at the desk in my dungeon, busy as a Dairy Queen fly, when out of nowhere came this rr-r-a-a-c-kk!

My first thought was, the termites have won; they're leveling the house before we can find a buyer with more money than brains. For my second thought (occasionally I have two in a row like this), one of our mice has got its little foot caught in a trap and is rr-r-a-a-c-kking around in the attic. A third thought being out of the question, I went back to my labor of making paper clip chains while waiting for inspiration to strike.

The next thing I knew, the rails holding the floor-to-ceiling book-shelves pulled out of the west wall, and the books from rows three and up came banging down on me, including the top shelf of the 20-volume set of *Harvard Classics* weighing two pounds per.

Fearing that her overstuffed cat, Lump, might have been injured in the avalanche, my dear wife, Lois, rushed in all atwitter. And she doesn't twitter easily. Digging down through the *Classics* until she came to my head, she said, "If you can hear me, wink your good eye."

If you can hear me? This woman would continue talking had my head been under water.

"I thought those screws were too short when you were putting up the rails...and you should have put those heavier volumes on the bottom shelf and the paperbacks on the top..." and yakety-yakety-yak.

But would she make these suggestions at the time? And spoil the fun? No way.

To continue, I take you now to the placement of Christmas lights on the tree in our yard.

"You hold the stepladder while I climb up and drape this string over the top branches," I remember telling this woman I

Playing Leapfrog with Porcupines

had taken for better. No sooner had I arrived at the top step, however, then over I went, ending up draped across the line fence. Luckily, the two strands of barbed wire stretched across the top were festooned with barbs of a length that went through my jacket and penetrated my human hide to a depth that kept me from falling to the ground and possibly being hurt.

Upon inquiry, her limp explanation was, "I let go of the ladder to untangle the next string. I knew you'd be mad if I handed them to you all messed." Better dead than mad.

The stepladder still usable, I used it to reach the loft in the shed where our daughter Shari had stored most of her frozen assets when she moved to South Carolina. Having bought a pet ostrich, I assumed she now wanted me to locate and transport her world's largest birdcage. While I am up there searching, this same woman took the opportunity to borrow the ladder to relocate the kitchen smoke alarm so it wouldn't go off every time she burns the toast. Upon finding the world's largest birdcage behind the world's largest loom, therefore, I am feeling around with my foot for the ladder...and no ladder.

After hollering myself hoarse to no avail, I then spot my good old reliable Murray riding mower within possible reach. With agility belying my age, I manage to lower myself and get both feet on the seat. Having been left in neutral, the mower now began rolling across the floor of the shed. Had I not been holding the world's largest birdcage, I might have done better. As it was, when the mower hit Shari's world's largest kiln, I went up over the cage and came down on the bench where I keep the antifreeze, motor oil, roofing tar, and stuff like that. It wasn't a pretty sight. Nor is the birdcage still the world's largest.

On the subject of riding mowers, for her birthday I bought my dear wife her very own cute little five horse. Although I have always been generous to a fault, in this case it was more to spare my big red Murray 11-horse from suffering the sticks, stones, stumps, and whatever else she can find to run over when she's at the wheel. Especially mole tunnel ridges. Even ridges that could have been made by nothing less than beavers. But she levels them like a bulldozer. If the movie people should require a no man's land, we've got the perfect location. All they'll have to do is sprinkle a few bodies around. And the way things are going, one of them could very well be mine.

Why this woman ran the garden cart into the back of my knees when we were gathering leaves to put on the garden still hasn't been explained to my satisfaction. "To get the cart closer to you" sounds rather weak, considering the kick she got from watching me ride the thing downhill until it hit the trash burner and dumped me out.

How does my dog, Brutus, get into the act? His size helps a lot. And we're talking about a dog that checks out what we are having for dinner by looking *down* at the table. My dear wife has a spoiled cat, Lump, whose perks include one of those electronic entrances that does everything but screen for rabbits, which she delights in bringing in for playtime, which she did only this week.

Released just inside the door and perhaps never having been inside a house before, the rabbit appeared somewhat confused regarding proper etiquette. Brutus, in his eagerness to show it the ropes, knocked over the cacti stand, dumping the sand into the floor furnace, then ran around the coffee table, over the sofa, behind the stereo, and into the bedroom to topple the Leaning Tower of literature on my nightstand. In hurrying to open the patio door to let the poor thing out, dear wife struck her best knee on the oven door, retiring her from the game and leaving me to collar Brutus and be dragged into the catch-all closet where the rabbit had taken refuge and where the ironing board toppled over on us. This separated dog and rabbit long enough for me to catch the ingrown hare (sorry) and take it to the brush pile behind the barn. I had to get my own dinner.

Remember when I went all out for her birthday and surprised my helpmeet with a pair of safety shoes to wear in the kitchen when she is making biscuits? Those biscuits were never heavier than the morning she stopped scraping toast to announce, "I

Playing Leapfrog with Porcupines

thought I might put another coat of paint on the house trim today."

What she was actually saying of course was, "I thought you might put another coat of paint on the house trim today." But to make her commitment look authentic, by the time I had got into my painting outfit she had already erected a scaffold.

I use the word scaffold lightly. What it was was a board resting on a potato crate at one end and two bricks lying edgewise on a turned-over washtub on the other end. As she had cunningly positioned the board with the rotted side down, I no sooner mounted this construction and got my brush loaded with black paint than I began painting a broad stripe down both window panes on my way to the ground. As my painting outfit and epidermis absorbed most of the gallon of paint, my dear wife could complain only of the dent I had put in her washtub.

One more bump in the daytime and I'll let you go.

For all my years, I never knew that in winter a car hood tends to come slamming down without warning. Like it came slamming down on my neck this winter when checking the antifreeze rating in my dear wife's car. And while I am trying to breathe through my ears, this woman came out for her daily emergency run to Wal-Mart and said, "Are you going to be under there all day?"

Had I been able to talk, I would have responded, "If you'll help me get the hood up, I want to show you something under here." But she got into the car, leaving me to get the hood up and realign my head without help.

How to prevent the majority of these bumps, I have only one idea—but making our community property public would be *so* embarrassing. If you have a better idea, please address it to me in care of Bloomington (IN) Hospital. I tend to be there more than I'm home.

Now you can go—if you haven't gone already.

Chapter 19

SUBJECT TO CHANGE—WITHOUT NOTICE

There's an old saying—so old, in fact, that not even I can remember it. No matter. It had something to do with the more things change the more they remain the same. The saying must have been based on our house. The truth is (and that's a switch in itself), our furniture gets more wear from being moved than it does from being used.

Remember the night I came home late, and so as not to awaken my sleeping beauty, I undressed by the light of fireflies romancing outside the window, tippy-toed over and collapsed on what should have been the bed? Only it was the vanity? And for the next three days I smelled like an Avon lady's sales kit in mid-August?

Well, the situation hasn't improved. Take the sofa. To save the wear and tear of moving, I'd put the thing on wheels if it weren't for motion sickness. Or the TV. If the wires would reach, I'd be out in the shed watching Vanna turn the letters, dear wife having exhausted every possible location in the house.

While seeing hubby search out the TV's new location gives her much enjoyment, the kitchen provides even more entertainment. Especially the old switcheroo in the cupboards.

Her finest hour comes with watching her married opponent reach for the bran flakes and bring out a box of Minute Rice. In his morning fog he doesn't discover the error until his selection has been raisined, sugared and milked—too late to waste on the dog. I tell you, gentle reader, there's nothing like facing a hard day's work on a hearty bowl of Minute Rice.

My Jubilee melons were nothing to shout about this year. How come? It's because I nourished them all summer with kitty litter instead of Miracle-Gro. And why would I do a stupid thing like that? It's because my dear wife dumped a sack of kitty litter into the bucket where I keep the Miracle-Gro.

Playing Leapfrog with Porcupines

"Maybe you can sell your melons as cucumbers," she said by way of apology. And maybe you've switched your heart and your gallbladder, I said, to myself luckily.

Not even my wardrobe has escaped the genes for change coursing through her veins, or wherever it is genes course. For evidence, I offer my robe, the one I toss on before daybreak to power walk Brutus, our 105-year-old dog, humanly speaking.

In a fit of compassion, dear wife decided that the robe was too thin for the morning air whistling across our Freedom, Ind., hilltop. It would be just the thing to cut up, however, and use for cleaning the oven, should she ever get around to it. In its place she proudly presented me with a robe she had made from what must have been an old army blanket.

This dear woman had even gone to the zoo and somehow got permission to use a gorilla for a model. The sleeves hang down to my knees, and I can reach the pockets only from a squat position. The squatting down I can handle; it's the squatting up that gives me problems, as the robe weighs at least 45 pounds. I won't try to estimate its girth, but I can't wrap the thing around me without getting a running start.

Or take my side of the bed, which should be private property, right? Especially when everything is in order, magazines stacked neatly on the left side of the nightstand, fiction on the right, Tums and Ben-Gay in the center, non-fiction piled orderly on the floor. Certainly no grounds for the ultimatum: "Get rid of that mess or get out of the way!"

Sure enough, the next time I was out of the way, I came home to find that she had assembled a bookcase from Wal-Mart and arranged my stuff so that I'm still looking for the book I was reading when she turns out the light.

This brings up another little matter, if you have a minute.

In slapping the bookcase together, she got the unfinished ends of the side panels up and the finished ends on the floor. To turn the finished ends up would require unloading the thing, but then the shelves would have the unfinished sides up. So there it is to this day.

The only thing in its favor, it coincides with the stereo cabinet dear wife assembled in our living room. Here, if you'll notice, as most visitors do, the finished back panel faces the wall and the raw side is plainly visible through the front glass doors. Make a point of it? I'd sooner run into the proverbial buzz saw.

If the inside of the house falls under the jurisdiction of the female of the species, the outside belongs to the male, right? Not at our theater of operations. Not when God has failed to provide trees in the correct number and in the right places.

The main attraction that lured us to these 13 hilltop achers (and I do mean achers) was the view. Our view today, however, has changed from White River, the lush valley and the little town of Freedom, to Virginia pine, blue spruce, and nux vomica (the tree that makes you want to throw up).

To be fair (I must not be feeling well), the fault is not entirely my dear wife's. Part of it goes to the state forestry people who sell trees and won't dirty their hands on an order calling for fewer than 200. And that, my friend, is twice as many as 100.

After dear wife had pointed out the spots and I had dug the 200 holes and lugged the water, she did her part by handing me the 200 trees to commit to the earth. Three days later, noticing that I had regained my faculty for walking upright (except while wearing the robe—remember the robe?), she ordered another 200.

If you are counting, this adds up to 400 trees for me to inter into the terra firma. And we are talking here of terra that happens to be as firma as the north side of the Alps. While I haven't had it assayed, I peg it at 80 percent clay, 20 percent limestone, with limestone being the most pliable of the two.

Finally (and about time, I'm sure you are thinking), guess what my dear wife gave me for my last (make that latest) birthday? Something practical, like a jug of liniment or a hose for draining my blisters? Nope. It was, in her words, certainly not mine, "a darling little sugar maple."

"Now you can make your very own maple syrup," she said sweetly—if you'll forgive a Tom Swifty.

To tell the truth (I must be sick) I don't expect to be around by the time this little hunk of flora begins to produce sap. And if you are concluding that it has produced one sap already, go ahead and conclude. At least I had the smarts to marry a woman who continues to supply me with material for these authoritative articles.

Chapter 20

TOOTH OR CONSEQUENCES

Although the issue has yet to be settled, I claim that the woman I took for better is the one responsible for my tooth trouble in the first place.

I had entered the living room on this particular night to find her on her hands and knees peering under the sofa. This being strange behavior even for her, I thoughtfully inquired if she had lost her marbles.

Ignoring the clever innuendo, she replied, "No, it's my thimble."

Servile hubby that I am, I helped her to her feet and said, "I'll get the yardstick and sweep the thing out."

If you have ever tried this at home, you no doubt know the results: popcorn, peanuts, Cracker Jack, the cat's little rubber ball, a long-lost earring, a nickel, and two pennies, not to mention—but I don't mind mentioning it to you—dust balls enough to build a sizable snowman.

For my next stunt I risked popping the rivets out of my hernia operation by moving the sofa away from the wall, after which my sadistic spouse gaily announced, "Never mind, it's right here on the end table."

In biting down on the yardstick, I loosened this tooth.

A fairly front tooth, the poor thing had already suffered the trauma of a root canal. (You may remember "Sailing Down the Root Canal," my educational article on the experience.) And I had been under the impression that after a tooth had been canaled, it would last a lifetime, if not longer. At least simply biting down on a yardstick shouldn't cause it to go antigodkin— or slaunchwise, to be more precise.

Now you know and I know that when your own proficient dentist farms out the job to an oral surgeon, you've got trouble— not the least of which could be that my jawbone might come out

Playing Leapfrog with Porcupines

with the tooth. I further speculated that postponing the removal of this rotten apple from my dental barrel might cause the other front apples to go down like a row of dominoes.

The anticipation of having a tooth pulled is enough in itself to make a man of my limited fortitude wish he had been born with a full set of dentures. Especially when a man's sadistic spouse prints in bold red letters the date of the execution (extraction, I meant to say) on a POST-IT™ and posts it on the refrigerator door, where a man will see it whenever he hears the butterscotch pie, the cherry cobbler, or the chocolate mousse crying out to be released from their cold prison cell.

On deadline day, the cause of my trouble bravely drove me to the office of the tooth-pulling expert, courageously steered me into the waiting room, where she hid her deep concern behind a copy of *People*. I was left to fill out a form asking how I would pay, did I have someone to drive me home (my next of kin, in other words), and how much did I weigh (a subtle way of determining whether they'd need help in carrying me out).

A nurse then escorted me the 13 steps to the electric (there I go again)—dental chair.

With the possible exception of expectant fathers in a waiting room, nothing compares to the tension of sitting in a dental chair listening to sounds emanating from the room next door. That *rattle* can be nothing less than a brace and bit coming out of the dentist's tool kit. There's the unmistakable sound of an upper tooth being removed through the top of the head. The *thud* has to be a body falling to the floor. And the murmur of conversation leaves no doubt that the dentist and his assistant are discussing disposal of the remains without emptying the waiting room. To say nothing of the chair occupied by the white-knuckled gentleman next door.

"And how are we today?" trills this exuberant young chap who finally comes bouncing into the room waving my X-ray and ending any hope that my appointment had been for *next* year.

"Yef geeb ugharr," I respond, the nurse having already minimized my speaking faculties to a trickle.

Maynard Good Stoddard

"That's good," chirps the chap, who turns out to be the dentist rather than a student observer, as I had placed him. "This being a root canal," he says, "the tooth will be brittle and may break off."

Without further ado, he picks up a pair of pliers and breaks it off.

"Are you all right?"

Just dandy, thank you for asking. How could anyone not feel just dandy with a root canal broken off and the roots still connected to the jawbone and the jawbone connected to the head bone and the head bone connected to the spine bone and the spine bone connected to the seat of his emotions?

Luckily, at this point I remembered the wise saying of—was it Solomon who wisely said, "The best way to counter an irritant is with a counter irritant"? Anyway, I'd give it a try.

Let's see, now...How about the night of my dear wife's Chef's Surprise? That dish delivered all the excitement of a slug race in July. Or her innovative peanut butter pizza? That not only stuck to the ribs, as she had promised, but to everything else on the way down. My rising hackles were countering the dentist's probing and prying already.

Then there's dear wife's association with the automobile...BINGO! Go no further, Maynard, you've hit the jackpot. Think about how she insists on sharing the driving "so I can relax." For reasons of health, I have yet to inform her that with her at the wheel I'm about as relaxed as a housefly in a swatter factory.

If the speed limit is 65, she is going to drive 65, come fog, sleet, hail, dark of night, over hill, over dale, over stumps, whatever. Then there's her unorthodox way of driving with one foot on the accelerator, the other foot on the brake pedal. Perhaps her ilk, or a sizable herd of her ilk, drive this way. I wouldn't know. I do know that she approaches a traffic signal at 40 miles an hour, slams on the brake, wastes a quart of fuel, and burns up a yard and a half of brake lining per stop.

Playing Leapfrog with Porcupines

Another tooth grinder (barring a dentist having his tools in your mouth) is the way she waits at a four-way-stop intersection until every other vehicle within sight has cleared, including a spavined horse pulling a load of hay. As for her keeping to the white line marking the edge of the road, you'd think that every other car had a contagious disease, spark plugitis, or fatal valve-in-head. For trucks, she generously drives off on the shoulder. "WIDE LOAD" alerts have her frantically looking for an open field. It matters not that her ashen-faced passenger all this time is left staring at a guard rail, a bridge abutment, or possibly a stray moose waiting to cross the road.

Although counter-irritated by this time to where forceps entering my inner ear could have gone unnoticed, to be on the safe side I thought about dear wife's reaction when the traffic light turns green. So as not to hold up the driver behind who may be trying to reach home with a half gallon of frozen yogurt before it becomes unfrozen, she puts her foot in the carburetor, as they say at the Indy track, and she's out of there. Unable to ingest this sudden flood of fuel, the poor engine begins to gag, cough, sneeze, belch, and finally throw up the excess, for which I, not she, have self serviced at $1.15 per.

I thus responded with little concern when the assistant asked me to raise my hunkers so she could slide a metal plate under me. Not until I awaken to the fact that this plate was wired to a gadget of dials, switches, and blinking lights does the message come through that the remainder of my tooth is about to be electronically dynamited.

But before I could get my legs organized and head for the door, the dentist said, "Are you okay?" And it is over.

My unique composure throughout the ordeal did not go unrewarded, however. Though the going rate for extractions had been quoted at 90 to 150 big ones, I got off for a measly $95. I also was given a packet of pain pills and a small quantity of tea bags, which I was to moisten, one at a time, and clamp down on to stop the bleeding.

My much-relieved wife drove home. On the white line. One foot on the accelerator, the other foot on the brake pedal. Stopping and starting at three traffic lights. I clamped down on a tea bag without moistening.

Chapter 21

LOW ON THE HOG

Coming into the kitchen from my morning labor of sanding a rusty paper clip, I said to my dear wife, "Where'd you get the dowel rods?"

"Those are breadsticks," she said. "I may have left them in the oven a tad long."

A tad! I couldn't make a dent in one of those things with my industrial set of dentures. Brutus, who has no trouble chewing kindling, took it out and buried it without bothering to try.

Now don't misunderstand. I love my wife as well as the next man. Loves his wife, perhaps I'd better add. And I certainly don't want to give the impression that she is totally unskilled with the skillet. If you should get that impression, that's your problem. I have enough problems of my own as it is.

It's not that I expected my bride to take the marriage vow with one hand on a cookbook or anything like that. But when the preacher said, "Do you promise to tell the truth, the whole truth, and nothing..." I'm sorry, I'm confusing this with another ceremony, which is easy to do. But what I'm getting at, along with the vow of loving, honoring, and cherishing, there should be something about the basics of cooking, feeding, and catering. Catering to hubby's tastes, for one thing.

In all the confusion, it never occurred to me that the bride would be serving the dishes she prefers. If hubby doesn't happen to prefer them, tough. He is certainly free to serve up his own. Or to get his McMeals elsewhere.

My dear wife, for one horrible example—let me rephrase that: For one horrible example, my dear wife has a passion for liver and onions. Onions I'll go for. But I draw the line at eating the internals of an animal. I even have trouble with eggs. It's just the thought of where they've been, if you know what I mean. But when it comes to liver—and I quote from the *American Heritage*

Maynard Good Stoddard

Dictionary: "Liver. A large compound tubular vertebrate gland that secretes bile...," which is enough right there to turn my delicate taste buds to the wall.

One of my favorite dishes is Beans Arkansas. You know, beans, chips of crisp bacon, and onions. She doesn't care for Beans Arkansas. I made it once, in '43 or '44, to show her how. I've been waiting ever since.

She is big on tacos. I hate tacos. As I tell her, "You might as well save the shell and dump the stuff directly into my hand; that's where it's going to end up anyway." We have tacos often.

I like things well done. She likes fish still flopping and steak so rare I've seen cattle hurt worse and live.

To be fair (I'm not myself today), my dear wife's rare genes could have been inherited. I suspected this early on when, to decide if I was worthy of their daughter's hand, and accessories, the parents had invited me to Sunday dinner. When the platter of chicken finally arrived at my station and I attempted to spear a leg that had escaped the brunt of the cooking process, it shot off the platter and onto the floor.

Not being an avid reader of Amy Vanderbilt's etiquette column at that time, it was up to me to decide whether to kick it under the table and take a stab at another piece or to rescue the thing and nonchalantly pick off the dog hair as if I'd done it a dozen times before. Fortunately, the dog came rushing over in time to resolve the issue for me.

How these genes for *trichinosis heartburnosis*, as they're known in medical circles, can be transferred to one daughter and miss the other one completely is "just one of those things," as geneticists will explain for a fee.

One daughter who looks upon a can opener as the world's greatest invention, got off on the wrong gene at age four by making her dear daddy an oyster cracker sandwich. Two slices of unbuttered bread with a dozen oyster crackers painstakingly spaced inside. And as she stood proudly by, dear Daddy had to get the thing down, praising its taste at every bite. Dear Daddy couldn't whistle for the next three days.

Playing Leapfrog with Porcupines

Today, she is the one who cooks a turkey with no curiosity for what might be stored inside, like a cellophane sack of its internal organs. She is the same one who dumped a can of cherries into a store-bought piecrust only to discover after baking that there were two crusts, separated by an unsavory sheet of waxed paper. Her mother finds no fault in her.

Our other daughter, who follows a recipe to the 1/8th spoonful and baking time to the quarter-second, is regarded as a weirdo. To those who cook by the seat of their pants, the squandering of her money on a library of cookbooks is tantamount to investing in nose flute lessons at Julliard.

My dear wife, by contrast, figures if she comes within a half hour of the cooking time called for, she's in the ballpark. And if one garlic clove is good, three garlic cloves should be three times as good. I'm writing to the SmithKline Beecham people to inquire if they sell Tums in bulk.

Something else that failed to cross my cluttered mind at the time I pledged alliance to my bride: when the wife goes on a diet, hubby goes right along with her. What he is served to sustain him is the same hare fare of lettuce and carrots, with a luscious hunk of raw cabbage for dessert.

When finally I noticed that my nose was beginning to twitch, I put my foot weakly down and grasped for something that would stick to my ribs. And do you know what that dear woman did? She made me a peanut butter pizza. It stuck not only to my ribs but to everything else on the way down.

Another little matter that came late to my attention: If she serves something to me that she doesn't serve to herself, I can depend upon its being at least four days old. "I just wanted to clean out a few things," is her explanation. And too often that also includes me.

After years of eating my dear wife's biscuits, I now take them for granite. You may remember me giving her a pair of safety shoes to wear in the kitchen when she is baking. Frankly, I'm trying to forget it. That's when I really put my foot in my mouth. (I could add that my foot would be tastier than some of

Maynard Good Stoddard

the stuff I've eaten. But in deference to the stuff that lies ahead, I won't add it.)

Heaven knows I have watered my garden with the sweat of my brow to put the finest of foodstuff on the table. My stuff, unfortunately, doesn't arrive at the table, without first going through the hands of the middle-woman. Did you ever hear of a carrot casserole? Or pickled beets so pickled they make your ears come together at first bite? How about potato salad made with yams? I'm thinking of installing a stomach pump right up there with the fire extinguisher and smoke alarm.

Oh, I know her rebuttal. How about the time you soaked beet seed in cider to give the beets an apple flavor? Or how about you planting potatoes on a hill so they'd roll into your basket when you cut off the bottom row? And how about the stuff you bring in that wouldn't make hog swill? (I wish she'd rebut that sometime so I could come back with, "You oughta know, you've made enough of it.")

Okay, so maybe my vegetables don't come up to State Fair quality. Am I at fault for being tender-hearted? I just can't bring myself to thin those little fellers that have worked so hard to push through our billiard ball clay soil. With two tiny radishes competing for the same spot, who am I to say this one lives, this one dies? One hour of making decisions like this can put a man on the couch for the rest of the day.

And is there anything more moving than two little carrots twined about each other? What difference does the eventual shape make? That's my closing argument—they're still 100 percent carrot.

My dear wife and I made up recently on our patio love seat, so called, while the sweat of my brow dried in the afternoon sun. In that subtle way she has of letting me know that I am right and she is wrong, she came out with a box of cones and a half-gallon of frozen yogurt.

"It's black cherry, your favorite," she said.

Playing Leapfrog with Porcupines

As usual, I allowed her to make a black cherry frozen yogurt cone. But as I was eating the last of it, what I took to be a black cherry turned out to be a June bug.

With a great restraint, I said, "I'd much rather it had been a black cherry."

"I don't know how that got in there," she cracked. "But just like the yam salad, you didn't eat enough to judge."

The love seat has been vacant ever since.

Chapter 22

MY NEXT DOG

The companionship of a pet in one's waning years can do marvelous things. I see the results in my own dear wife, who remains reasonably under control by stroking Lump, our spoiled, overstuffed white cat (which she has cleverly named "White Cat") that claims her lap whenever she sits and turns obscenely belly up (we're talking about the cat, now) beside her when she lies down.

My good old dog companion, however, is now chasing angel rabbits in a much fairer land than this. Although Brutus was a bully, always wanting—and having—his own way, I miss him. And after a long and lonely year, I know he'd forgive me if I welcomed a replacement. But this time, *I* will be in command. *I* will lay down the rules. And my new dog can like it or leave. Period.

Friends, of course, have sought to ease the loss of Brutus by offering to unload a puppy on me. No way. Nor have I taken a dog off the street. This time I am going to a pet shelter and pick out just the right dog. Should it require more than one trip, so be it.

If I come to a cage where this dog sticks his muzzle through the bars, I may stop and let him lick my hand. But that's it. He'll be wasting his saliva, I can tell him that. Nor is he going to con me with that plaintive, lost-puppy look. Oh, I suppose if he whimpers a plea that goes something like, "Please, sir, will you get me out of this stir? There's a rumor going around that my future here isn't all that bright. And I'll be your friend for life. Please, mister..." then I might take the dog home. But only on a trial basis, understand.

The first thing this dog is going to learn is, no begging at the table. Let him turn those soulful eyes up at me all he wants; I'll pay no attention. This dog is going to learn discipline right from

Playing Leapfrog with Porcupines

the start. Of course, if he gives me that look and then puts his paw on my knee, indicating terminal malnutrition, that's a different story. No one wants to see a dog keel over right there at a bountiful table when a few pieces of chicken or maybe a chunk of cake might save him.

And late-night snacks are out. I'm drawing the line here, too. It's for his own good: weight control, strong teeth, shiny coat, and all that. If he is awakened by the aroma of burgundy cherry frozen yogurt, he can go right back to sleep. Unless, of course, trying to eat with his paws on my shoulders becomes tedious. In which case I might break down and give him the last half of the dish. But no more than that, definitely.

As for sleeping on our bed, not this dog. I'm putting my foot down here as well. Once he hits the scales at 100 pounds, he's on the floor. Except for cold nights, of course. Our floors are somewhat drafty. And how can a man sleep with a dog lying on a drafty floor whimpering his farewell before rigor mortis sets in?

Which reminds me: this dog is not coming in every time he yips. Dogs were made for the outdoors. Let him scratch on the door all he likes; he'll be wearing out his nails for nothing.

If his yips turn hoarse, of course, that's something else. Not that he's going to the vet at every sniffle. Not this dog. Dogs in the wild have a way of healing themselves, and this includes the common cold. Should the cold be uncommon, however—sneezing, coughing, and redness of eye that tells you he could go at any minute—only then will I lug him to the car, hoping to get him to the clinic in time.

And if this dog is slow on the tick when it comes to learning tricks, it's back to the kennel, I can tell him that. Not that I expect him to shake, sit, or roll over right off the bat. I'm asking only that he show promise by coming to the doggie dish when he's hungry, wait until we leave the house before sleeping on the sofa, and learn that he's safer under the bed during a thunderstorm. In which case I might have a little patience.

Maynard Good Stoddard

This dog will not be luring me back to the woods on the pretext of having treed a moose. Oh, perhaps if I haven't had my power walk for the day...but I'm definitely not following him through the brush—unless he barks "HELP," that is.

One more thing. No rounding up a posse or phoning an ad for the "Lost and Found" column if this dog disappears for an hour. A dog needn't be right under your feet every minute. If the time stretches to two hours, however, that's another matter.

When he finally does show up, he'll be in for a good lecturing. And while I'm at it, no more digging up the lawn under the pretext of hunting for moles, no more sleeping in the salvia bed to escape the sun, no more using the birdbath for a bathroom, and so on.

Unless, of course, the poor thing comes home exhausted, perhaps even limping. But after I have fluffed up his bed and examined his feet, this dog is going to hear from me. If he gives me that look that in canine language means "I'm sorry," okay, I might let him off the hook this one time. But no more. And he'd better remember it.

Chapter 23

LEND ME YOUR EARS

How do you reveal to your dear wife that she not only has become hard of hearing, but that she's also beginning to mumble?

She, on the other hand, doesn't hesitate to suggest that it is me who couldn't hear "a sonic boom if it were in the next room," as she so quaintly puts it. Me, imagine. But to keep our marriage from going belly-up at this late date, I laugh it off as only a desperate defense for her own auditory deterioration.

Actually—and this is confidential—my only concession to the "silver citizen" generation has to do with my sense of smell; it's pretty well shot. In fact, and this is just between us, I couldn't smell a skunk if it were sitting on my lap eating garlic. But if my dear wife knew this, no telling what she might be trying to pass off at the dinner table. What she gets away with already is murder.

Anyway, I have approached her hearing problem tactfully, if I do say so myself. Other husbands might have come right out with something like, "By the way, dear, do you realize you're becoming deaf as a lamppost?" But I went to the Spencer-Owen Library to explore the reason why she is becoming deaf as a lamppost, and how we might avoid our current pattern of conversations:

Me:	It looks like rain.
She:	What?
Me:	I said it looks like rain.
She:	I didn't hear you.
Me:	What?
She:	I said I didn't hear you.
Me:	IT LOOKS LIKE RAIN!
She:	You don't have to shout.

Maynard Good Stoddard

Me: What?
She: Oh, forget it.

Now, I'm not suggesting—lest it put my eternal well-being in jeopardy—that our Maker in making man made a mistake. But it would have been thoughtful to have the human ears continue to grow with age. With a cutoff date, say, at around age 65, or at least before they reached the size where they'd be piling up on the shoulders. But earflaps of maybe 8 or 10 inches would certainly have saved conversations from being sprinkled with witty retorts such as "Hmm?" and "What?" to the more profound "How's that?" and "Come again?"

The library, however, didn't provide as much help as I had hoped. "Conductive deafness from earwax blockage", I understood, although I had to look up *conductive*. "Sensorineural deafness from fluid pressure in the labyrinth" didn't mean a thing. (I thought the labyrinth was somewhere in Italy.) About the only explanation of my dear wife's condition that made sense was "the hearing mechanism gradually degenerates with age, and about one-fourth of the population over 65 need a hearing aid." Also within my intellectual grasp was the revelation "to an adult who has started to become deaf...high tones are less audible than low tones, and the sounds *s, f, and z* are not heard at all."

So where did that leave a man of my gentle nature? To tell my dear wife to go soak her ears was out. Definitely! To limit my usual witty remarks to words without the *s, f,* and *z* sounds could very well bring my usual witty remarks to a screeching halt. There would be less risk of our marriage ending up in small-claims court, I decided, if I girded up my loins and suggested to Dear Wife that she was ripe for a hearing aid.

But whadaya know, folks, when the idea presented itself, I lost my nerve.

We were watching a movie on Channel 4—watching the action but guessing at the dialogue—when she said, "If that's as high as the volume will go, the old set needs an overhaul."

Playing Leapfrog with Porcupines

The volume was loud enough at least that I had to reply, "What?"

"The volume is weak! The old set needs an overhaul!"

The perfect opening for me to inject, "It's your ears, old girl, that need an overhaul." But instead I meekly called the repairman.

For a mere $114.85 (the bill is now thumbtacked above my aging bride's sewing machine), he tinkered at the back of the set, put up a new aerial, and at 9 cents a running foot ran in a new coaxial cable guaranteed to bring in stations from outer space. Thoughtfully, he piled enough extra footage behind the set to reach the barn, should we ever choose to watch television out there.

When this did nothing to increase the volume, I took the bull by the tail and looked the issue square in the face, or however that goes.

"Why don't you try a hearing aid?" I suggested.

"What?"

"A hearing aid! Why don't you get one?"

"Why don't you?"

"I'm sorry, I didn't hear you."

"WHY DON'T YOU?"

That's the way I thought it would be. Me first. Always me. I had no need for bifocals, but I was the one who had to lead the way. I was the one who saw three steps off the patio when there were only two. I was the one on my hands and knees when she came out and asked what on earth I was doing.

"Looking for buckeyes," I explained.

"You're under the elm tree," she pointed out. (She was hearing all right at that time.) "The buckeye tree is over there."

"I've read that they now have hearing aids for dogs," she went back to jabbering. "We ought to get Brutus one."

She was right about that. Although we still had a "Beware of dog" sign posted, for Brutus to detect an intruder now, the intruder would have to intrude on his tail.

Maynard Good Stoddard

I should have said, "Why don't you get Brutus a hearing aid and you could share it?" but I didn't think of it until the next day. Instead, I said maybe I would try an implant, like Ronald Reagan's. I could have saved time by repeating it then, but instead I waited for the inevitable.

"What?"
"An implant!"
"Can't what?"
"What?"
"You can't what?"

These situations get even more serious when she asks me something like would I care for tea with my dinner. I tell her yes, tea would be okay. But I don't get tea. And why don't I get tea? Because I asked you, she says, and you didn't say. So I have to haul myself up from the table and make my own tea.

Another inconvenience associated with her hearing problem has to do with the phone ringing.

"Telephone," she'll call out. (She has even poked her head in the shower to tell me that the phone is ringing.)

"What?"
"The telephone!...Can't you hear it?"
"Of course I can hear it."
"Well...aren't you going to answer it?"
"It could be for you."
"ANSWER THE DARN PHONE!"
"Yes ma'am."

The only reason I let her get away with this at times is to build her confidence. If I should ever fall victim to her hearing handicap, I'm sure I would appreciate the same consideration.

As for the TV volume being below her hearing ear waves, I solved this problem thanks to a commercial hawking a gizmo called the "Sonic Ear." Designed like a pocket radio, the earphones to be clamped over the head are connected by wire to this amplifier. With the earphones in place, according to the lingo, you can "hear a pin drop from 50 feet away." What actually sold me, however, was the line "It works so incredibly well you literally won't believe your ears."

Although I had no use for this thing, to make Dear Wife feel at ease, I ordered two. And what do you know, folks, they actually work. So you'll find us at night watching TV with these contraptions clamped over our heads (that's one head apiece) and looking like a couple of astronauts awaiting the countdown for the sofa to take off for the moon.

Whether the Sonic Ear deserves all the credit, I can't say. My wife's hearing has definitely improved. Just last night as I went to the kitchen to answer the phone, I muttered under my breath, "That's all I'm good for around here." Upon which she immediately responded, "You can say that again, buster!"

On second thought, it might have been the low tones, which are easiest to hear. I probably shouldn't have growled.

Chapter 24

SNAKE IN THE KITCHEN

My wife doesn't scream very often. When she does scream you kind of get the idea that something may be amiss. Like maybe a snake in the kitchen. Which there was.

Of course, I didn't know that until after risking a rupture and whacking my best knee leaping from my desk to rush out and see what might be amiss.

"Look," she gasped, pointing to the window.

No question about it, hanging from the curtain rod above the kitchen window was this snake, its head swinging back and forth and its beady eyes checking out the strange surroundings.

My wife had already backed over the cat and hit her funnybone on the microwave. In hurrying to protect her, my hip joint caught a corner of the table, which provided me with a little time for meditation.

I must admit, I have never met a snake I liked. Even the garter variety is enough to have me dropping the hoe and heading for the house. And in my youth I outraced many a blue racer. Those two varieties constituting all I know about identifying snakes, what we were entertaining here could very well be a viper, asp, copperhead, even an adolescent anaconda, the kind that hug you until your eyes pop. I had read that a friendly snake has round eyes and a poisonous snake's eyes are slits. But I was not especially eager to check that close.

"Can you see if its eyes are round or slitty?" I whispered.

"Not from here," she said aloud. And just the way she said it I knew the temperament of the snake would have to be determined by another method.

"I read about a woman sitting at the dinner table in India who felt a cobra wind around her leg and she told a servant to place a bowl of milk on the floor and the snake left her leg and went for the milk."

Playing Leapfrog with Porcupines

"What if this one isn't a cobra?" asked my wife, who knows even less about snakes than I do. "Besides, I gave the last of the milk to the cat."

I was about to suggest that the snake might go for a cat full of milk, when I spotted the broom standing in the corner. The only problem, the corner happened to be the one by the window from which the snake was now glaring at me. To reach the broom would require me to scuttle across the floor and strike my healthy knee on the drawer handle beneath the oven door of the range. Which I did.

With the broom in hand I held the whisk part up to the snake, hoping he might climb aboard. Where we would have gone from there I hadn't worked out. Probably turned it over to my wife and run to open the door. The situation, however, never came up, as the snake only hissed at the broom and turned to see what else I might have to offer.

Noting by now that its eyeballs were round and trusting in my recollection that round eyeballs meant nonpoisonous, I found the courage to move the broom around and raise the ruffle on the curtain. It was a mistake. What I had in mind was maybe a snake of, say, a foot to a foot and a half in length. This one was coiled around and around the curtain rod and then around and around its coils. When I dropped the broom, the handle landed directly on the big toe of my left foot. It still hurts on rainy days.

Content with doing all the damage it could do for the moment, slowly the snake unwound and leisurely began to crawl across the wall toward the back of the sink. When all but a foot or so of its five feet, by conservative estimate, had disappeared, I grabbed hold of the last six inches to pull it out. For what reason I have no explanation. Luckily, it kept on disappearing.

So now, the sink having no back to it, somewhere amongst the pipes, the buckets, the bottles, the odds and the ends and the just plain junk, we also had a snake. To leave it there would of course be to never know when entering the kitchen where you might encounter the thing. I had even heard of a snake coming into a bedroom to share the electric blanket. One of us, therefore, had to rout this reptile out and route away from the bedroom.

"It's your cleaning stuff," I pointed out to my wife.

"You'd know better than I what should be moved. What to look into. And so on."

We finally agreed to remove the stuff alternately, she taking out an object, then my turn. She going first, as it was her cleaning stuff. Thus by ducking in and out, we had everything removed but the mop bucket in the corner. And it was my turn. If you ever saw a mop bucket snatched up in a hurry, that was it. And if you ever saw a man whack his head on the sink ledge coming out of there, that was also it. And I had jarred my brain loose from its mooring all for naught. No snake.

However, after my vision cleared, I spotted a 4x4-inch square hole that a former tenant had cut into the wall behind the sink. If it had been for something besides a snake entrance, its purpose escaped me.

We couldn't be altogether certain, of course, that the snake had found its way out. Hadn't I read that most snakes are nearsighted? What if this one had gone right past the hole and was now reposing on the floor behind the sink? Not only did we leave the junk out for the rest of that day, to be on the safe side we also looked under the bed, around the bed, and in the bed that night before climbing in ourselves. A little past midnight, when the cat jumped onto the bed, I was out of there before my wife could say, "It's only the cat, where do you think you're going?" I had to get my own Band-Aid to close the gaping wound in my knee that had failed to clear the wrought iron nightstand. My wife, a bit nearsighted herself, said it was only a scratch.

The next morning, after another search finally convinced us that the snake had indeed let itself out, I plugged the hole with insulation and stuck a piece of tape across it. And that was that...until that afternoon when I flung open the cellar doors.

Yep. Along the concrete ledge heated by the sun shining on the metal doors, there lay our snake, stretched out to its full five, or six even maybe seven, foot length.

Playing Leapfrog with Porcupines

What happened after that was almost too fast for the human memory to record. I remember dislocating my wrist disengaging my hand from the door handle, and I took time to scrape my good knee across the corner of the door before departing for the patio. From this vantage point I saw the snake, now heading for the line fence, cut off by Brutus, my foolhardy dog. With Brutus sparring with the snake's head, Lump, my wife's cat, seized the opportunity to sink her claws into its tail. The snake promptly rolled itself into a ball, no head or tail showing. My dear wife, to show me up, as promptly dashed out with the broom and rolled the snake over to its original objective, the line fence.

I spent the rest of the day on the patio with my wrist in a solution of Epsom salts and my eye on the fence. And again, that was that...until the following day.

When I am home, Brutus and I share the chore of walking down our hill to the mailbox, he carrying up the junk mail. Never before had he so much as dropped a single sweepstakes envelope or letter asking for money. Today, however, on our way back, eureka! (accent on the eek). There lay the snake sunning itself on the grassy slope. By the time Brutus had investigated and discovered that the snake was sound asleep, I had twisted my ankle and backed into a freshly pruned forsythia.

Brutus, the crazy mutt, actually went up and touched noses with the snake, which woke it up and set it in motion, it going one way, me the other, bum ankle and all. We haven't seen the snake since...to date, that is.

That same weekend, however, we were at Clifty Falls State Park and by coincidence, after hobbling up to the Nature Center, I saw our snake's identical twin. It was in a cage labeled, "Black Rat Snake." Above the cage hung the sign: "HARMLESS."

That shows how little they know about snakes.

Chapter 25

MY WALK WITH "LADY" LUCK

Why is it, one might ask—I being the one—that Luck runs in some families while in other families she walks, with a limp.

Take my family, if you're not particular.

We had this aunt who contracted tuberculosis from licking Christmas seals. Another aunt on her way to Wednesday night prayer meeting was run down by a rusty police car and died of lockjaw. One of our nephews was drowned in a watermelon-eating contest. During the Great Depression the only job an uncle could find was to sit behind the front window of an Italian restaurant and eat spaghetti and meatballs from 10 a.m. to 5 p.m.—with an hour off for lunch.

You may remember the cousin—actually a cousin twice removed, removed the first time to Leavenworth, the second time to Sing Sing—who was released from the latter institution a few days before Christmas and stopped off in New York City to pick up a few gifts for the folks back home. The poor fellow ended up with three fractured vertebrae and a ruptured spleen from falling down a flight of hotel stairs with an armload of Gideon Bibles.

Why his brother suddenly decided to leave for Africa has never been cleared up. The consensus was that it had something to do with his walk through a neighbor's back yard one night and stumbling over something which he couldn't identify. Picking it up and carrying it home, under the kitchen light he discovered that it was an armload of wood.

After several nights of such occurrences, the neighbor came over to discuss the mystery of how come his woodpile was depleting so rapidly while cousin's was holding its own, if not gaining. Cousin left for Africa the next morning.

Luck's casual concern for our family is perhaps no better exemplified than by the abortive efforts of Thomas Alva Edsel,

Playing Leapfrog with Porcupines

our entrepreneurial uncle. For his initial effort he chose to concoct the soft drink, "6-Up." He followed this with a man's deodorant which he labeled "Left Tackle." Uncle Edsel then spent 10 years writing *The Hunt for Blue November.* It sold a grand total of two copies, one being returned for a refund, a banana peel still in place as a bookmark between pages two and three.

Luck and I got off on the wrong foot as early as my tenth birthday with my parent's gift of a pet lamb. It was allergic to wool. I never could catch the poor thing.

Having suffered so many slings and arrows of outrageous misfortune since that time, I find it hard to know where to begin.

How about this spring, when I fired up the rototiller after its winter hibernation. I remembered to shove the gear thing into "F" for forward, which got us to the garden. But when I shifted into "R" for Rototill, I nearly got myself rototilled full length. It's the "T" that starts the machine to tilling; the "R" is for Reverse.

I know what you're thinking. You are thinking that such a mishap by no means compares with the kind of luck that caused Uncle Quonse to be drowned in the Flint River while being baptized. (You remember Uncle Quonse, named after the Quonset hut because of his long head, due, it was said, to his mother having run into a mailbox the week before he was born.) The way it happened, the preacher said he couldn't be baptized with his hat on. Uncle said he wasn't going to take it off, not in that cold water. The preacher said yes he was. And somehow in the struggle poor Uncle Quonset stepped out too far and the current got him. Remember?

Anyway, Frivolous Luck continues to delight in her little shenanigans. Especially now that the knight of my youth has shed his armor.

Three months after recovering from cataract surgery, I got a cataract on the artificial lens. The ophthalmologist of course calls the condition by another name, but he doesn't know Fickle Luck like I know Fickle Luck. Or Susie, for that matter.

Maynard Good Stoddard

What a ball the old girl (Luck, that is, not my eye doctor) has with the accouterments accompanying senior-hood. Eyeglasses, in particular—or spectacles, if your hood is as senior as mine. Remember the time I was mowing the orchard and a low hanging limb on the dwarf Red Delicious swept off my bifocals and before I could bring my big red Murray riding mower to a stop, their mangled remains came spitting out the grass chute? My optometrist, requiring some ready cash, recommended replacing the remains with trifocals, at a humongous price per focal.

In the first place—or is this the second place? my memory…but you already know about my memory—trifocals aren't as easy to get used to as falling off a log. But falling *over* a log, or over the pattern in the living room rug, for that matter, is right down trifocals' alley. They also delight in showing two steps where only one step exists, leaving it up to Capricious Luck to have me stepping on the one that isn't there. Which increases momentum to the point where descents can best be described as spectacular. Like the one in the bank building where I took this girl with me. As she was still sitting on my lap at the foot of the stairs, to make light of the incident, I said, "You might as well get up, this is as far as I am going."

All of which is beside the point, the point being that no sooner had I learned to negotiate stairs with these three-tiered jobs, than Floozy Luck proveth that pride indeed goeth before a fall.

Now, I am what is known as a sound sleeper—I wake up at the slightest sound. But before surrendering myself to the arms of Morpheus (not to be confused with the arms of Lois, my soulmate), I place my costly specs atop the Learning Tower of Literature that adorns my nightstand.

Here, as they say, the plot thickens.

My awakenings most often can be traced to Brutus, who sleeps on the floor at my side of the bed, and who has this hobby of collecting fleas, and celebrates the acquisition with a series of triumphant thumps that rattle the windows. On this particular

Playing Leapfrog with Porcupines

night he attained such success that I finally rose up to see if I could kill him without disturbing my Sleeping Beauty. That's when I felt this *thing* on the back of my neck.

With an instinct born of sheer terror, I knew what it was. For the past two weeks the décor of our walls had gone to spiders, and I'm talking about spiders you couldn't get into a coffee mug without a shoe horn. To dislodge this critter, I shrewdly threw my neck out of joint and then joined Brutus, who rose up and dumped me back onto the bed.

Seeing the outline of this hideous interloper against the white sheet (off-white, to be honest, quite a ways off, to be precise), I grabbed up one of the books made convenient by the commotion, and began belaboring the beast.

It was at this juncture that my dear wife turned on the bed light, and in a voice a wife reserves for those occasions when she's awakened at 2:15 a.m. by hubby beating on the bed with a book, said, "And just what the billy heck do you think you are doing!"

You know, folks, it's rather difficult to formulate a plausible explanation when one is staring down at the remains of $179 worth of trifocals.

The good news is, Licentious Luck may at last be smiling upon me, however faintly. The breakthrough occurred at a motel in Port Clinton, Ohio, this summer. Coming in out of the bright sunlight, I failed to notice that some pranksters had removed a section of the plywood flooring leading from the dock area to the rooms, and I ended up at least four feet down surrounded by 2x6s and steam pipes. The motel people not only canceled the cost of our two nights there but also paid all of my hospital bills.

If your family happens to be one in which "Lady" Luck runs, I realize that this may not seem like much. But to me it's a step in the right direction.

Chapter 26

UP ON THE ROOFTOP AND DOWN

Falling off a roof is not something you learn overnight. My own apprenticeship—you may remember this—began with tarring the seams on the roof of our front porch and my dear wife "borrowing" the ladder for the emergency removal of 5-year-old ivy from the siding. And I ended up behind the spirea with a bucket of roofing tar in my lap.

Although the next 11 years were devoted mainly to digging tar out of my bellybutton, I have still managed to spend quality time adjusting to rooftop situations. Only last week, for one situation, I mounted the old aluminum ladder to see if I could locate the source of a leak that had begun watering the flower pattern in our living room rug. Five minutes later, wind blew the ladder down.

No problem. Dear wife at the time happened to be mowing what we refer to as our front lawn. I had only to attract her attention to my predicament. Who can possibly avoid noticing a man stranded on a roof shouting and waving, then throwing a glove, then the other glove, then creeping to the very edge of the peak, removing his shirt and letting it sail off in her direction? (You thought I was going with it, didn't you? Sorry, but I managed to grab the antenna post at the last second. Better luck next time.) And did my dear wife at last look up and say, "Oh, I do believe that my dear husband is in trouble—I must race up on the mower and inquire"? In a pig's eye. I might as well have been shouting at the shingles, waving at the neighbors, and draping my shirt over the chimney.

Had the mower not run out of gas when it did, my headstone might very well read: "Roofed to death, July 11, 1992." Her limp excuse for not routinely checking on my welfare was, she saw the ladder down and assumed I had gone inside to watch the ball

Playing Leapfrog with Porcupines

game. If my hands hadn't been covered with tar at the time, I don't know what might have happened.

A leak in the roof is about the only incentive for going up there. Unless it's to hit a high voltage wire while installing the antenna. You could go up there for the view, of course; it all depends upon who lives next door. You won't be going up there for your health, that's for sure.

I know how it is with you young, biceptical hubbies, you'll be couch-potatoing some evening, and you'll turn to your dear wife and say, "Tomorrow, I promise, weather permitting, I'm going up on our roof and fall off." The next day the weather is perfect for falling, but you keep making excuses: you can't find the liniment, where was that board you were going to use for a splint, and like that, until it's too late. Falling off a roof by flashlight is not wise.

The roof over our original four rooms and path failed to provide the leak incentive. The room we added, did. The room was an afterthought. Not mine. Actually, I didn't think much of it. But my bride of the Roosevelt era (no, not Teddy, for heaven's sake!) soon began campaigning for a bath to replace the path. And closets, to eliminate the need for hanging her clothes on hooks, which tended to give her dresses the appearance of having been hung on hooks. Which was particularly noticeable at the all-important occasion of giving our older daughter away. (We sold the younger one).

This addition, luckily, had a nearly flat roof. So according to the carpenters' code, it had to be covered with roll roofing. And water on nearly flat roll roofing has no place to go but through—if it can find an opening. Which our roof soon provided. More fortunate yet, the opening happened to be over one of the three closets usurped by the person who had been clamoring for an added room.

Had it been above the shower, no sweat, of course. Rainwater is billed as beneficial to the hair. But a songwriter has yet to come up with a romantic ballad about "Raindrops Keep Falling on My Dear Wife's Wardrobe."

Thus, for the past 11 years plus, I have mounted the roof after every rain. And after each dismount I have assured the one with the wet dresses that, by golly, this time I had it, no question about it. But the next time it rained, she would begin to ask questions: why? when? and how long, oh Lord, how long?

After one boisterous wet spell, I paid two men $250 to resurface the roof, the clumsier of the two men taking advantage of a weak spot to fall through. To conceal the blunder, he filled the hole with an extra five gallons of tar.

And it did stop the leak. After that, the roof didn't leak, it ran a stream. And the stream consisted of 60 percent tar. So instead of rainwater converting my dear wife's clothes to off-white, they were so far off white they were black.

I had always thought I would leave my dear wife an estate consisting of stocks, bonds, cash, credit cards, and maybe a yacht or two. Then I thought of some hand-kissing vulture luring her to the altar and making off with the whole wad. My third thought (three in a row established a new record for me) was to invest the whole bundle in a brand new, leak-resistant, perhaps even leak-proof, roof over the addition.

With this last thought in mind, I phoned Larry Morley, a local Jack-of-all-trades, to come up and lay a new roof over the old roof.

"Never mind bringing a helper," I said. "I haven't spent the last 11 years of my life up there without knowing my way around."

My dear wife having already regaled Larry on my attempt at draining the basement into the pond and through a slight miscalculation draining the pond into the basement, he said it wouldn't add greatly to the labor charges if he brought his 12-year-old son.

They showed up the next morning with $318 worth of materials and Larry's workman's compensation policy. Which was akin to running out on the track before the start of the Indy 500 and soliciting the drivers for burial plots.

Playing Leapfrog with Porcupines

Surprisingly, except for sawing a new opening in my pants, I surprised everyone with my professional performance. Until it came to rolling out the roofing.

"I'll hold the roll from back here," Larry said, "and you roll 'er out."

Why didn't he say something before I rolled 'er off the edge of the roof, was my first question after regaining the power of speech. He said if I had been up there the better part of 11 years, I should have known the location of the edge of the roof.

Had it not been for the fiberglass overhang, I might be faxing this article down from "up there," or sending up smoke signals from "down there." The good news is, I missed going into the cistern by a foot and a half.

Funny, the thoughts that will cross a victim's mind at times of such crises. On the way down I thought of organizing a rock group and calling it The Collapsed Lung. This left little time for midair adjustments, but enough so that I managed to land on a freshly tended flower bed. I've landed on softer beds, of course, but any bed you can walk away from is a good bed, as World War I aviators used to say.

Hearing the commotion, my dear wife ran out and with deep concern screamed, "Look what you've done to my marigolds!"

Had I been up to it, I would have replied, "A woman with the sense God gave a retarded goose should have known better than to plant flowers where a man falling off the roof might land." But I couldn't spare the breath at the time.

In fact, I still walk with a slight hitch in my south leg, and my neck is kinked at an angle that gives the appearance I'm trying to spot the planet Pluto.

If current therapy fails, I may have to fall off the roof from the other side to get straightened out. I'll let you know.

Chapter 27

BABY, IT'S COLD INSIDE

Of the several ways of heating a house—solar, wood stove, oil furnace, baseboard electric, and applying a blowtorch to the sofa stuffing—the latter has begun to look more and more appealing.

Over my dear wife's dead body (at least that was her argument), we had started off heating this termite convention center we call a house with a wood stove. (Or a stove that burns wood, to be accurate; a stove made of wood might be trouble.) I chopped the wood, I lugged in the wood, I kept the fire going, I hauled out the ashes, I cleaned the chimney. But who said the stove was too much trouble? Right. And who was cold all the time. You've got it. When I took this woman for better or for worse, I didn't know that among the worse was a bloodstream clogged with ice floes originating in her feet.

My blood flows freely at a room temperature of 68 degrees. Hers grinds to a halt below 74. The stove being located in the kitchen, the temp here had to be pushing 80 before she would enter another room in the house without coat, scarf, mittens, and earmuffs. So why didn't I move the stove into the centrally located living room? She would whimper. My feeble excuse was that without a chimney in the living room it might be somewhat of a problem. Then we'll replace the wood stove with an oil furnace, she decided.

Did you ever try to argue a home heating problem with a woman who is already a tad blue around the gills? Especially when the woman is wearing earflaps?

"I'd rather smell wood smoke than the stench of fuel oil," was my No. 1 protest. "Maybe you would, but thanks to your precious wood smoke, my lipstick plant is breathing its last," she rebutted.

Playing Leapfrog with Porcupines

I told her she could buy her lipstick—there was no need for her to grow her own.

Letting this go in one ear and out the other, which in her case is no problem, she said, "And my amaryllis blossom is already three weeks overdue."

"Wood ashes are good for the garden," I countered.

"Maybe chimney soot would be even better," was her off-the-top-of-her-head reply. Way off the top, I might add.

"And we'd have to get one of those unsightly fuel tanks that tells the world we can't afford electric heat," was my rejoinder.

"And what has your old wood pile been advertising?" she countered, having lifted one earflap to catch my rejoinder.

The outcome, of course, was ordained before the foundation of the world. And the Sears people, already in business by that time, and well aware that a husband's chance of winning one of these domestic tiffs ranges from zip to zero, had an oil furnace already loaded by the time my dear (make that costly) wife called. And they had it installed beneath our living room floor before I could come up with yet another rejoinder. I installed my beloved wood stove in the shed, beneath a sheet of plastic.

Now, I'm not placing the blame entirely on the furnace. Nor am I submitting that it was cholesterol that clogged the fuel line. I *am* asking why it is that when we have an expensive new appliance to brag about, it is "ours," but the minute it stops applying, it suddenly becomes "yours" —as in "Your furnace isn't working again."

The furnace works fine during daylight hours, no problem. Or I could turn the thermostat up in mid-August and the thing would leap joyously into action. What it is waiting for is the coldest night of the year, when the master of his castle—as some hopped-up bachelor poet in the Bahamas chose to dignify a man's humble abode—is snugly ensconced in bed. Then and only then does it decide to show old master who is really in command of this moatless termite terminal.

"Let's give it another hour or two," I suggest, burying my head beneath my pillow.

Not deep enough, however, but what I still can hear her say, "By that time we'll be stiffer than boards. The flashlight is up on top of the refrigerator."

Taking the subtle hint, I haul out of bed, pull an old fleece-lined jacket trimmed in fuel oil over my pajamas, locate the flashlight, and in my haste to enjoy refreshing midnight air, forget to turn up the collar of the jacket. The blizzard thoughtfully does it for me. And to make my walk to the furnace pit even more invigorating, the blizzard also fills my slippers with snow.

Removing the sheet metal cover, I ease myself into the pit. Lying on my back, I squeeze beneath the pipe running to the chimney. Get stuck. Back out. Remove my fleece-lined jacket. In bare pajamas I now worm my way to the front of the furnace, reach through the accumulated cobwebs, and hit the "Reset" button.

To my surprise, the furnace starts, belches a cloud of smoke and soot in my face, and quits. Upon regaining partial vision, I try again. Same result. Scrunching back under the pipe, I pick up my jacket, cover the pit, and stumble into the house, which I find a pleasant five degrees warmer than the outside.

The crunching sound upon again reinstating myself in bed comes not from the mattress, as I first suspect. Turns out to be from the soot in my pajamas. I am ostracized for the rest of the night.

I'm also on my own for breakfast, because the cook refused to depart from the bed until she can no longer see her breath.

After calling the repair people, I go to the cereal shelf and indiscriminately take down a box. Cereal is cereal, right? They're all high-fiber, low-cal, great taste, crunchy, wunchy, munchy, and so on. Right?

Wrong. Not this time, anyway. Thanks to slugabed's unique method of organization, the cereal I chose turned out to be a box of Minute Rice. Which I didn't detect until after I had sugared, raisined, and milked. And you know me—I sure wasn't going to let it all go to waste. Nothing, I say nothing, will set a man up for the day quite like a hearty bowl of uncooked Minute Rice.

The repairman arrived on his double-time emergency run at 7:30 that evening. While dear wife and I held our respective breaths (primarily so that we could not see them), he clanked and banged around until 9 o'clock, presented me with a bill for $168.72, and said, "Sorry, I can't help you."

As I too was wearing earmuffs at the time, I didn't catch all of his explanation. Something about the fuel oil gelling before it could reach the furnace. And we should stick our electric heater in the pit and hope for the best.

So I took our only source of heat and stuck it in the furnace pit and hoped all night. To no avail. Returning the next day and finding us still alive, the repairman wrapped the fuel line with heat tape, replaced the nozzle and filter he had installed the night before, and, no doubt attempting to relieve his conscience, charged me only for the parts.

I could tell you how I was talked into investing in baseboard electric heaters to turn on when the furnace turned off. And how our electric bill the next month rose from an average of $32 to $182. And how I put a "Use at your own risk" tag on the control knobs. And I could go on, but this typing isn't easy for someone with the head of a blown-glass unicorn stuck to the index finger of his right hand.

The way it happened, to atone for all the trouble she had caused me by exiling the wood stove to the shed, my dear wife had planned to surprise me with this unicorn for my collection. Unfortunately, due to inflexible fingers (the furnace having conked out again), she had dropped the unicorn and its head had departed its body. Thus I found her in the kitchen, awash in tears, trying to reunite the two pieces.

"My hands are too cold," she whimpered.

The surprise element by this time pretty well shot, I volunteered to apply the glue and hold the head in place until it dried. "It dries in only a minute," dear wife sniffled as she shuffled off to bed until the repairman could reschedule an appearance. (It seems that in retrieving our space heater, I had turned off the heat tape.)

And for once, by golly, she was right. No more than a minute later the unicorn head was cemented to my finger. The glue tube offering no directions for the removal of a blown-glass unicorn head from the human finger, I may have to be so adorned until the thing wears off.

In the meantime, I'll be working in the shed. A unicorn head on my finger won't be too much of a handicap when it comes to putting up a chimney.

Chapter 28

SNAP, CRACKLE, AND WHAM!

I don't mind things that go bump in the night so much as I mind things that go *snap, crackle, crash, whine, whimper, scratch, thwack,* and *crump* in the daytime. Oh yes, and *wham.* We mustn't forget *wham*—much as I'd like to.

Why anyone in his right mind (which is open for debate) would move to this hilltop convention center for termites in the first place is a good question. Actually, it wasn't in the first place, it was in the second place. In the first place I wanted to stay in our snug apartment in Indianapolis, where the only disturbing noise was the sound of the morning paper hitting the porch roof. But when the lathered up real estate person assured us this view represented the highest point in Sweet Owen County, we fell for it. What the real estate person failed to mention, this is also the point where lightning forms.

My bride of yesteryear, however, was overjoyed at this serendipity, as she had been brought up to view electrical storms as merely God's way of jump-starting the cowardly. Thus while bride is at the window observing whatever it is lightning does, I am under the bed with the dog and cat, making more noise than both of them.

As of this writing, our termite B & B still stands, but only because it once was surrounded by five towering black locust trees. I say once was, because there are now but two towering black locust trees. The others?...yup, wiped out by God's handiwork. And upon each of these thrilling occasions, in addition to the racket, lightning followed the tree roots to the water line, where half the volts made a hard left to burn out the hot water heater in the root cellar, the other half going gaily down the 248 feet of well pipe (at nine bucks a foot) to wipe out the jet pump. We now have both appliances on standing order.

After the remaining two trees get theirs, it's good-bye house, as we sometimes jokingly call it. It is hoped, however, that the mattress may spare the gathering under the bed. As for the termites, they may have to go to the barn. Or maybe the neighbors will take them in. I'd hate to see the poor things go hungry.

One thing in our favor is termites don't make noise smacking their lips while chewing up the supporting timbers. The mice are not so considerate. They have this exciting game of storing dog food pellets in the master's summer shoes stored in the attic. The amount of plaster a contestant can bring down between the walls on each trip from kitchen to attic, where the shoes have been stored in a box to keep them out of harm's way, also counts heavily in the scoring.

After the little fellers move out in the spring, the walls remain silent for—oh, sometimes for an entire week. Then a clumsy starling chick falls out of its nest under the eaves. And does it fall to the ground for the cat's amusement? Never. It falls between the walls, from where it begins sending up distress shrieks that are answered by every matronly bird within the township limits.

"You've got to do something!" yells bride, after two days of trying to do housework with fingers stuck in her ears.

"Such as?" I queried. Upon getting no answer, I pulled a finger out of one of her ears and said I'd try dangling a worm on a string in hopes it would grab hold and I could pull it up. Dumping asbestos insulation on the squawler to give it an allergy that would force it to come up didn't work equally well (if you can figure that out, let me know). By day three we were longing for the days when mice were screeching their toenails down the plaster.

"Either it goes or I go," was dear bride's tempting threat on day four.

"How about running a garden hose down there and performing mouth-to-bill resuscitation?" I suggested.

Playing Leapfrog with Porcupines

That shut *her* up, but the chick squawked for another day and a half. I like to think the mother then came and lifted her bumbling baby like a cat carries its kittens, bill to back of neck. If I hadn't shut up my bride she'd have said, "That's ridiculous!"

Then there's Lump, her obese cat, who isn't satisfied with the nightly noise of scratching on the La-Z-boy, clawing the sofa, and shredding the clothes hamper. She is only honing her talons for the bagging of a mouse, a mole, a bird, a rabbit or a chipmunk, with which to pay for her board and room by delivering the thing through her private entrance as an offering for our table. Eat the victim herself? She wouldn't dream of it. Not when she can get a can of high-priced store-bought food every time she opens her yap.

Just this week I'm at my desk punctuating up a storm when she comes in with this live chipmunk, which she deposits at my feet and goes over to lie on the rug, her duty done for the day.

"There's your lunch, old master of the mountain," if I interpret her attitude correctly. "You can bake it, broil it, or barbeque it, but as for me, I'm too pooped to be interested."

This leaves me with the choice of having a chipmunk for a house pet or drawing on a pair of gloves and trying to run the uninjured little varmint down. Not only uninjured but now hyped to a speed of at least 20 miles per hour. The path I wore making a circuit from the cubbyhole I call an office to hallway to kitchen to living room to bedroom and back to cubbyhole will be in the carpets long after I'm gone (an event that's not far off, the way things are going).

Had this cavorting little critter not firmly established its fangs into a finger of my glove when I finally nailed it in my cubbyhole window, we might be going around yet. I'm holding my breath that my dog Brutus doesn't drag in a moose to liven up the place the day the cat comes in from hunting empty-mouthed.

Speaking of Brutus, we are speaking of a senior citizen animal that has honed his repertoire of commands and pleadings until he can make more sounds than a ruptured bagpipe. I refer to a *woof* the second he hears my eyelids go up in the morning, a *whine* if I don't leap imediately from bed, a *whimper* of desperation, then a *howl* that says you can let me out *now*, buddy, or take the consequences. Upon stubbing my toe on the end of the bed, a family tradition, we howl in unison all the way to the door (no; not my toe and I, my dog and I).

Which brings us to my dear wife. There is no sweeter sound to a man forming sentences at his desk than to hear through an open window the sound of her working outside. Except when she's mowing the lawn with his brand new bright red 11-horse Murray mower. It's like trying to form sentences on a firing range. *Whing*, she's just hit a stone...*whang*, a fallen tree limb...*whung*, a stump.

Until last Thursday I felt free to dash out and express myself concerning her carelessness in not removing the obstacles before running my brand new bright red etc. Murray mower over them. I further pointed out that I operate the cherished appliance over nothing but the most tender grasses.

Because the front wheels have a tendency to leave the ground when mowing up the hill that forms our front yard, I handle this tricky assignment myself. And once before mowing over a few twigs from a locust tree, I got off the Murray to pick them up. But not before wisely turning the mower sideways to the hill and turning the front wheels upgrade.

How the thing turned itself around, I haven't figured out. But I was picking up the twigs and humming happily to myself (I seldom hum to anyone else), when my brand new bright red 11-horse Murray shot past me at about 40 miles per hour. I, naturally, dropped my twigs and started to run after it. But as I can now do only 35 miles per hour, I soon gave up. And had to stand there and watch it pick up speed as it approached the board fence bordering the road.

I did get one break. My beautiful mower *whammed* one of the posts head-on. Otherwise, it would have gone through the fence, over the road, and disappeared down the embankment on the other side. In which case, we'd probably still be looking for

Playing Leapfrog with Porcupines

its remains. As it was, it took out the post and two sections of fence.

The mower still runs, although with a concave front end. As for the headlights, they are now just right for hunting coon. As far as I can see, that's the only advantage of having a mower hit a fence post.

My dear wife is out mowing right now. So far, I've heard only two *whumps* and a *thwack*. Oh, oh, there goes a *crump*. Oh well, what's another stump in the life of a mower?

Chapter 29

HOUSE BY THE SIDE OF THE ROAD

When two people of conflicting genders are confronted with the question of taking each other for better or for worse, it should be within the bounds of ceremonial ethics for one of the participants to stop proceedings at this point and ask a couple of pertinent questions of his own. Namely, "Worse than what?" and "How bad will it get?"

Much as I dislike dragging my dear wife into this, she is a fair representative of the opposing sex when it comes to deciding issues that the law of nature rightly left in the hands of the male of the species. High on the list of these issues is where the couple should live.

Take me (which would be OK, I'm sure, with you-know-who), for example. In my capacity as subservient husband I have been dragged to—let me count—exactly nine houses and two apartments. And that isn't counting the house trailer. Nor am I counting the housecar, which was once our abode for a proposed journey from Bradenton, Florida, to Mexico City. It's a sickening story, so I'll keep it as short as possible.

It began like this. Taking advantage of my euphoria over selling a poem to *Liberty* magazine (for a nifty 20 bucks), my dear wife stated that because my literary career had become firmly established, we would borrow $1,500 to put with the 20, buy a housetrailer (today's mobile home) and take off for Florida. Here, in a matter of, oh, say six months, my writing would make Hemingway's look like an eighth-grader's essay on what I did on my summer vacation.

And I, like a dummy, fell for it.

Actually, she was right about the six months. My writing did so well in only that short time we had to sell the car. Either that or break our habit of eating.

Playing Leapfrog with Porcupines

Left now without wheels—except for those on the housetrailer, resting on blocks at a trailer park in Ann Maria Key—we had no way of returning to our beloved Michigan, Mother's applie pie, the American flag, and stuff like that. When schools opened, we had the trailer towed to Bradenton, where Michael (5) could do his coloring under the supervision of a kindergarten teacher. Nikki (4) still would be cutting out paper dolls on her own.

You must understand that my dear wife had been born with at least five quarts of vagabond blood in her crankcase. To be without wheels was for her like going shopping without her purse. And somehow in her little pointy head the idea had fermented that our next destination would be, of all places, Mexico City.

And as bad luck would have it, one day while prowling through the jungle behind Bradenton Trailer Park I stumbled upon what I at first took to be abandoned rest rooms. Upon closer inspection, it had wheels. Badly as we needed wheels, we weren't *that* desperate, I chuckled to myself.

At least I thought it was to myself. Unfortunately, this used-trailer salesman, who happened to be downwind at the time, came crashing through the brush before I could make my getaway.

"How would you like to buy 'er?" he gasped.

"Buy 'er? What is 'er—or it?" I wisely inquired.

"That, my friend, is living quarters built upon a Velie chassis...a great car in its day." (I would learn much too late that its day had been in the early 20s, and a common expression of that day had been, "If the hood is up, it's a Velie.")

"Here," he said, "let me show you the inside."

Together we pried open the side door. And there, reading counter-clockwise, I beheld a pop cooler, a floor-to-roof "kitchen" cupboard, the front seat, a second kitchen cupboard, two-burner Coleman stove, sink, clothes closet, wall-to-wall bed across the back, another clothes closet, kerosene heating stove, and back to the side door.

"Will she run?" seemed a reasonable question.

He said she was running when he took her in on a trade. And when was that? Six years ago. We went out and he raised the hood. Vines were climbing out of the cylinders.

"Tell you what I'll do," he said, holding me by the arm. "If you get 'er home, send me three hundred dollars."

Well, I've been talked into a lot of dumb things in my day, but taking on that Thing (as it came to be called) and trying to nurse it to Mexico City by far outweighs all the others put together. Getting the first encouraging backfire from the engine took exactly a month to the day. My only contribution had been new spark plugs, the rest being left to Art Martin, a park resident with a mechanical bent, who had accepted the challenge and after the second week labored only for the satisfaction of seeing the Thing in motion.

In the meantime, dear wife was merrily going about the feminine chores of sanding, painting, washing, soldering, hanging curtains, and writing to her mother for the remainder of the canned goods we had left with her (which turned out to be a barrel—I'm not kidding—a barrel of peaches). The kids, catching her enthusiasm, couldn't wait to hit the road. It remained for Cookie, our nondescript dog, to put the project in proper perspective. The tow truck had no sooner deposited this automotive heirloom on the street in front of our trailer than he ran up and christened both rear wheels. His canine ESP must have told him what lay ahead.

Although the engine consistently smoked, the radiator even in cold weather did a marvelous characterization of Old Faithful, and the top-heavy body emitted more grunts and groans than a sumo wrestler, it would be the 25-year-old tires that turned this otherwise horrible experience into a nightmare.

So why didn't we start off on new tires? Because, as the tire man said, after using the Braille system to check the size, "Man, you won't find passenger car tires in that size this side of Greenfield Village."

"Then I'll put on truck tires," I said simply, as it turned out.

Playing Leapfrog with Porcupines

"Not on those two-and-a-half-inch rims, you won't."
"Then I'll put on wider rims."
"On those wood spokes? Don't make me laugh."

What made him laugh was when I told him we were heading for Mexico City.

"Mexico City!" he said, after he'd stopped laughing, "You'll be lucky to get out of town on those tires."

Undaunted (one can't very well daunt with a wife, two kids, and a dog urging him on), the next morning we were off. The many sad faces among the park populous brought a lump to my throat, which dissolved immediately upon realization that watching the Thing being towed had become the park's favorite spectator sport. The one cheerful face belonged to the park manager—a rumor had circulated that he had tried to bribe Art Martin to tow our home directly to the city dump.

Wouldn't get out of town, eh? That's how much the tire guy knew. We got...oh, it must have been at least five miles (the odometer didn't work), and no family provider ever looked into the rearview mirror upon a homier scene. There was Michael on the bed improving his mind with a comic book; Nikki on the bed trying to get her doll away from the dog; and dear wife, still clinging to her fantasy of reaching Mexico City, on the bed with her arsenal of maps, brochures, charts, and our itinerary, which now included Mardi Gras on the way and Grand Canyon coming back. If you're going to Mars, why not take in the moon on the way?

So much for domestic tranquility. The minute I heard the explosion and felt the Thing lurch toward the ditch, with quick thinking I said to myself, "Something's wrong!" As it was, the right rear had been the first to celebrate the tires' silver anniversary with a bang. And what the family provider looked back on now were two screaming kids, one howling mutt, and one wife's staring wild-eyed at a "living room" floor where pots, pans, and crockery rose out of a sea of catsup, mustard, mayonnaise, cereal, no-minute eggs, and uncanned peaches.

Maynard Good Stoddard

Tying Cookie to the back bumper of our house by the side of the road, we flagged a bus to Tampa. Bought a truck tire and corresponding tube. Arrived home in the dark. Discovered that Cookie had somehow found the fiberboard back panel edible and had edibled a hole large enough to squeeze through and was sweetly asleep on the bed. (The reason we reserved punishment was because his diet of late had consisted mainly of canned peaches, convincing us that a dog that won't eat canned peaches can't be very hungry.)

A phone call the next morning brought Abe Martin to the scene. And with all the enthusiasm of a sailor with a salmon can bailing out a torpedoed battleship, he mounted the truck tire on our cringing 2½ inch rim.

"You let 'er down," he said, backing away. "I'll see how she looks from over here."

So I let 'er down...and down...and down. When the tire reached a dimension of 2 inches high and 12 wide, I joined Art.

"Maynard, you won't get 50 miles with that setup. I hate to take your money," he said, taking my money.

The Firestone people in Tampa, where we replaced the left rear, were not this optimistic. "You won't get out of town, man," was their somber prediction. When I arrogantly informed them that we had already traveled 40 miles on the other truck tire, you'd have thought from their reaction that I had paddled a canoe across the Pacific.

Once safely past the city limits, I still drove like a man expecting to be served with a subpoena. After another ten miles I began breathing out as well as in. Before long I was accepting the growl of the transmission, the rattle of the fan, and the rhythmic grinding from the rear end much as the owner of a stationary house accepts a banging shutter or dripping faucet. By the time we hissed, rattled, and banged through Tarpon Springs I no longer worried about the various rackets. What now concerned me was that a member of this cacophonous chorus would suddenly quit making noise.

Playing Leapfrog with Porcupines

What quit first turned out to be one of the 2½-inch rims; the poor thing was split down the center by the truck tire bully.

With night approaching, as night often does in the South, we were desperate to find something to block up the axle, as I had nothing but a bumper jack to raise this Smithsonian refugee on wheels. Blocking material not being indigenous to Florida roadsides at that time, a weed-infested cemetary half a mile down the road left me no choice. I hoped that in the gloom the fat-cat tourists whizzing past wouldn't notice the "WILLING ELIJAH JOHNSON/December 6, 1851-October 11, 1909" inscription on the prop holding up the right rear section of our bedroom. (Let me hastily add that I replaced the prop straighter, and with fewer weeds than I found it.)

Hitchhikers carrying signs along Route 19 traditionally were looking for a ride to 'NEW ORLEANS" or 'TAMPA." I would be carrying a rim, after every leg of 50 miles or so, looking for a welder. And welders were no more indigenous to Florida than was blocking material.

How we made it to Tallahassee remains a 20th century miracle. Here, the transmission decided to have some fun by switching gears; shove it into first and it might go into high, or more sporting yet, into reverse. For this reason, among others, we parked on the outskirts of the city, hoping to go through before the morning traffic.

But we started late. And it was raining. And the cab roof leaked. And our appearance was further impaired by the pans over our heads, their handles fastened in the rolled-up windows. And we hit the very center of the city, complete with traffic lights and eagle-eyed policeman, at the height of rush-hour pedestrian traffic.

Where we got off on the wrong foot was in not lurching to a stop until the Thing, with radiator faithfully shooting off steam, straddled the crosswalk. This left pedestrians the choice of crossing in front or behind. I wished later I had opened the side door and charged them to go through and see how the other half lived.

With the light finally changed, the already irate policeman waved me through. What happened then had to do with our sleeping arrangement: parents on the full-size bed, Michael on a cot in the aisle, and for Nikki we unbolted the front seat and turned it around so she would be a part of the converted bedroom. In our haste on this particular morning, however, in turning the front seat back to its original position, we had forgotten to anchor it by sliding in the bolts.

Shifting into reverse, the Thing leaped forward, the seat and I went over backwards, with me lucky enough to catch the steering wheel with my toes. So once again our house remained by the side of the street until I could convince the Tallahassee police that I wasn't trying to be smart by driving past an officer with my feet holding the wheel.

The distance between Tallahassee and New Orleans on that particular highway was 404 miles. Divide 404 by 50, the approximate distance we went between rim splittings, and you can understand why I begged for a week in New Orleans to allow my back to straighten and skin to reform over my knuckles. Leaving New Orleans, by a vote of one to one (the kids abstaining), we turned north, my argument being I'd rather try to nurse the Thing back to Michigan than risk this top-heavy fossilized crate on the mountains of Mexico.

For all of the dismal miles on that leg home, we did experience one highlight to lift our spirits: we actually passed another vehicle. As we continued to gain on our prey and the kids began yelling encouragement, I "put my foot in the carburetor," as they say at the Indy track. And by the time we went belching past in a cloud of steam and black smoke, we must have been hitting at least 35 miles per hour. The fact that the other vehicle turned out to be an off-the-road stump-puller did little to tarnish our high spirits. But our spirits would be tarnished soon enough.

Rates on the front of this ram-shackle toll booth read:

Playing Leapfrog with Porcupines

Trucks	60 cents
Buses	50 cents
Cars with trailers	40 cents
Cars	25 cents

A ramshackle attendant came out, peered through the smoke and steam, walked around the Thing, came up to my open window scratching his head and said, "I sure don't know what to call it, son—how about giving me fifteen cents?"

Homecoming would prove to be even less uplifting. My dear wife's mother, upon hearing the Thing cachunking up the driveway, came rushing out to view the accident. When she saw her loved ones emerge from this—this "motorized monstrosity," as she would label it—we had quite a time keeping her from falling. And being president of the local chapter of the Women's Christian Temperance Union, she had not more than recovered when Cookie came staggering out the side door drunker than a goat. The last of the canned peaches had fermented.

As I mentioned when beginning this saga, in tallying our many and varied dwellings since I married my journeyman spouse, I'm not counting our housetrailer or the Velie. I think you can see why.

Chapter 30

POWER WALK

"Dr. Louis Sullivan and his wife power walk three miles a day," I said to my own dear wife through a hole in the morning paper where I had clipped the address of Credit Cards Anonymous.

To no surprise, she recognized Dr. Sullivan as our popular Secretary of Health and Human Services. What surprised me was that she had been listening. And for surprise number two, she peeked through the hole and said, "Why don't we give it a shot?" And even rambled on, something about my excess weight, my blood pressure, my cholesterol, and my bad temper.

What I had in mind, of course, was doing something about the persistence of her own baby fat. I also had noticed that Brutus, my dog, had cut his exercise regimen from jumping fences to picking up fleas.

"I can't power walk in high heels," my dear wife's first complaint.

"Imelda Marcos would envy your collection," I pointed out, to no avail. So it was off to Spencer to buy a pair of power walkers. After she'd talked me into a pair too, the total bill came to $84.60. Poor Brutus would have to wear what he had.

On our Big Four road, anything more than a school bus and maybe a pickup at the same time is considered a traffic jam. Without fear of traffic, we thus could walk briskly a half-mile to the curve and the half-mile back, giving us a grand total, for starters, of one mile of brisk walking. Right? As I pointed out to dear wife and Brutus when descending the driveway, unless we walk briskly we might as well remain on the couch with our feet on the coffee table. (Actually, Brutus remains on the couch only when we're away, and we have yet to catch him with his feet on the coffee table.)

Playing Leapfrog with Porcupines

The reason we got off to a relatively slow start could be laid to my having noticed on a recent visit to Washington that most joggers carried weights in their hands. Assuming that this was to exercise their arms rather than for self-defense, we had stopped by the shed. For dear wife I chose a gallon can of antifreeze and my tool kit, while I took on the sledge hammer and the hydraulic jack. With Brutus running ahead, we made it clear to the road and perhaps 30 feet beyond before deciding that we would postpone the exercising of our arms until our legs had been perfectly toned.

Once the weights had been deposited, we really hit our stride. All the way to the big maple tree. After we dragged Brutus away from there, he took off through the brush on the other side of the road with his nose to the ground. Five minutes later we heard that urgent bark he has indicating he has just treed a moose.

While my other companion waited, I followed the racket down swales and over dales, through Canadian thistles, poison sumac, and thickets of briars to where I came upon Brutus happily excavating a hole that had been dug by the grandson of the woodchuck that had walked off the Ark. He was glad to see me. I tried to keep in mind that he reportedly is my best friend as I power walked him back to the road and back to the house— where we later found him on the couch.

On my return, I found dear wife coming up the drive. Power walking her back to the road, we really now went into high gear. Just the two of us, man and wife, homo and sapien, chins up (that's one for me, two for her), setting out to overcome flab, cholesterol, blood pressure, and all other obstacles to health, home, longevity, the flag, Mom's apple pie, and all good stuff like that.

I had somehow failed to remember, however, that ours wasn't the only dog along the road.

One of the Millers' dogs had been named Little Henry because his deceased father had been crossed or double-crossed, by a Shetland pony. Little Henry, however, was little no longer.

Maynard Good Stoddard

In fact, when he put his paws on my shoulders, I noticed that we were about the same height. While I was trying to unload the beast, Baxter, the Abrells' dog, came up to greet us.

Baxter is a basset hound, one of those dogs said to be born under a bureau—they can't grow up, so they grow long. Little Henry got down off my shoulders to prove his dominance over Baxter. Dukes, Miller's three-legged dog, seized the opportunity to get in a few licks for himself (leaving us to speculate that Baxter might have been making fun of his handicap).

To me, this was a normal everyday doggie free-for-all. When it was over they would all go off together to tree a moose. But dear, compassionate wife, of course, had to wade into the melee to straighten things out. By the time she had got Little Henry tied up and patched up the relationship with Duke and Baxter, I was asking myself if that $84.60 might not have been better applied to a treadmill.

But at last we were off again, man and wife, etc., lowering our cholesterol, loosening the steam valve on our blood pressure, and "larding up the land," to quote a humor writer by the name of Shakespeare. We might even have powered our way past Abrell's house without stopping had not dear wife noticed that both the sun and half-moon were in the sky at the same time.

"How come?" she said, stopping to gaze skyward. "The moon is lighted by the sun, right?" That's right, I said. "Then why isn't all the moon lighted? You took astronomy so tell me that." So I told her. (I would tell you but you probably wouldn't understand it; I wasn't sure of it myself.) Anyway, by the time we got started again I had ground my teeth down to where I might never be able to eat corn on the cob again.

At least we now had clear powering all the way to the bend in the road, our turn-around spot. Oh, yeah? Not when Abrell's "cute" white-faced steers are in the corral. And, oh, look! One is coming up to the fence to be petted. When the cute beast shopped short of the fence ("the poor thing is a little shy"), dear wife, of course, had to open the gate and make the final approach.

Playing Leapfrog with Porcupines

How far we and Baxter and Duke chased those four cute capering critters before finally getting them penned in Strouse's barnyard, I can only guess. And I'm conservatively guessing about four miles. Doug Dyer trucked them back to Abrell's corral for a mere 25 bucks.

On our way home, my dear wife's bad knee went out.

"I'll get the wheelbarrow," I politely offered.

"Don't be silly," she said.

"How about the garden cart?"

She didn't answer.

With her arm around my neck, we began our debilitated walk homeward, appearing to all the community that I was bringing my wife home from an all-night bash.

Power walking a mile should be completed in, I believe, something like 10 minutes. We made it in an hour and a half.

The good news is that I lost three pounds. What my blood pressure might register, is another matter. In my current frame of mind, it's best not to know.

Chapter 31

FITNESS ON THE FARM

Have you heard about the grandmother who was told by her doctor to walk ten miles a day and after three weeks her family didn't know where the heck she was? Well, you've heard about it now. But let's say the dear woman had had the smarts to walk five miles out and five miles back. What would she have accomplished? Productively, I mean.

Exactly.

This goes for the guy sweating on the treadmill who could just as well be treading grapes for grape juice. Or the would-be Schwarzeneggers huffing on a rowing machine when they might be trolling for bass. Or how about the muscle maniac who risks popping his bellybutton lifting weights when he could be lifting a sack of potatoes onto the wheelbarrow?

Which brings me to our 13 "achers" here at Freedom, Indiana. There's nothing like a little acherage for productive exercise. And some days I get so absorbed by it that the next thing I know my wife is patting my cheek and asking if I know what day it is.

The aerobic people have this exercise of bending down and straightening up—down and up, down and up—without picking up a doggone thing. Not me. When I bend down it's to pick up a boulder Dear Wife wants rearranged in one of her four rock gardens. One time it was to rearrange the 48 quarts of canned tomatoes on the bottom shelf in the root cellar that were clashing with the peaches and had to be exchanged with the plums on the top shelf. Or it may be any number of brainstorms equally beneficial to biceps expansion.

Aerobic experts wouldn't think of beginning their efforts in futility without first "warming up," then "cooling down" after having accomplished nothing. We men of the soil warm up and cool down without giving it a thought—especially if we are

Playing Leapfrog with Porcupines

married to someone of the extreme opposite sex (to coin a phrase from Dave Barry). On winter mornings we usually warm up by bringing in an armload of wood for the kitchen stove so the room temperature will be tolerable when the one who scrapes the toast finally comes stumbling from her den. We cool down at the end of the day by slipping exhausted between sheets suspected of coming directly from the refrigerator crisper.

Aerobic practitioners practice a ritual they have cleverly labeled "Arm Circles." It consists of waving the arms in circles. Are they signaling? No. They are just standing there, waving their arms, and looking stupid. But when a farmer waves his arms he is likely turning old Betsy into the barn to exercise his fingers, unless he has a milking machine. Or he is shooing the hens out of the road so that the entrée for the evening meal won't consist of Chicken Under Toyota. Or, as in a case with which I am more familiar, he could be trying to call attention to the fact that in repairing the board fence along the road, he has managed to get two boards nailed with this head caught between them.

A man with a spread even as small as 13 achers never "runs in place." He runs with a definite goal in mind. One of my healthiest runs of late had the goal of catching a riding mower that was going downhill unattended after I'd dismounted to pick up a tree limb in its path. And one of our neighbors recently got in quality running time by crossing the pasture lot wearing a red flannel shirt, unaware that a bull had jumped the fence to romance one of his cows.

Another excellent opportunity for "running for cause" is what we earth people refer to as "chasing those blasted pigs out of the garden again!" If the garden were lush with truffles, that would be one thing. But pigs interested only in uprooting everything verging on ripeness is quite another. There's nothing quite like chasing them all over heck's half-acre to tone up the old leg muscles—as well as the old vocal cords (unless children are present, of course). As for carrying weights to tone up the old arm muscles at the same time, what better than a length of two-by-four to brain one of the porcine rototillers if proximity permits?

The "Arm and Leg Lifter" is another formal exercise we people of the soil perform without dwelling upon it. Patching a leak in the roof above the kitchen, I have found, follows the formal formula to a T. There's the lifting of the legs when scaling the ladder. There's the lifting of one arm to grasp the ladder rungs while the other arm is hoisting a 50-pound tub of tar. Once I'm on the roof realizing the advantage of this opportunity, I usually go back down the ladder for a brush to apply the tar. I often go down a second time to get a hammer and chisel to open the confounded tub. And after finally spreading a coat of tar between me and the ladder, I tone up my chest and abdominal muscles by sliding down the antenna pole.

The experts' exercise for abdominal toning, of course, goes under the heading of "Abdominal Curl." This calls for the curlee to lie on his back and raise both knees to his chest. Which, as always, accomplishes nothing productive. But when I, for one, lie on my back and bring my knees to my chest, it's to curl my abdomen under the pipe in the furnace pit and then raise up to hit the restart button. The beauty of this is that I may be offered three times in a single night this opportunity to heave myself out of my abdominal curl position in bed to reap the more substantial reward of curling under the pipe.

I could go on. So—if you've got another minute—I will.

In getting exercise through heating the house, I'll take wood any old day. It's so hard to carry an armload of fuel oil. But instead of getting that wood by means of a hard-to-start, noisy, smelly, polluting chain saw, there are still some of us who prefer the blessing of cutting our firewood—and being warmed by it twice—using a good old crosscut. And should a tree we fell happen to fool us by falling directly on the henhouse, there's the added advantage—if you'll forgive another personal incident—of chasing the survivors all over Abrell's 40-acre pasture field.

As for performing the "full body stretch," a man of the soil is presented numerous opportunities in his run-of-the-mill day. My

Playing Leapfrog with Porcupines

favorite is having the stepladder slip when I'm cleaning the gutters. I once managed to hang from the gutter for a full five minutes—strengthening my vocal cords at the same time—before dropping to the ground and flexing both ankles and knees so thoroughly that I gave them the next three days off.

Giving credit where credit is overdue, gravity has been one of my most faithful allies in the building of my biceps. The day my dear wife usurped the ladder and I came sliding down the porch roof to find it missing did wonders for toughening up my fingernails, as well as arm and leg muscles. I can't say as much, however, for the forsythia bush where I landed. It didn't bloom for the next two seasons.

The distance one falls, however important, is exceeded in exercise value by how one lands. This plays an important part in determining what section of the body will be benefited. With constant practice at what springboard divers would call an aborted "one and a half with full twist" —which only recently I executed while pruning the apricot tree—I have what must be the most exercised tail section in all of Sweet Owen County.

Whether I will live forever, thanks to these many wonderful exercise opportunities, only time will tell. I just read of a study showing that from 30 to 40 percent of heart-disease deaths probably could have been prevented if the couch potatoes had only exercised.

Well—not to be hard-hearted—it's their own fault. They should have lived on a farm instead of a couch. Like me. If one day, through no fault of my own, I *should* happen to go, at least I'll go healthy.

ABOUT THE AUTHOR

Released from a wartime job in Indianapolis, I packed my wife, Lois, and our two little kids into a house trailer (now upgraded to a mobile home) and took off for Bradenton, Florida, to launch my writing career.

I would spend many dreary months tied to the dock, however, before shoving off. So dreary, in fact, that the morning we needed a 22-cent quart of milk for breakfast, we could only raise but 18 cents. That afternoon, in the normal mail of rejections, a strange blue envelope stood out like the proverbial sore thumb. The editor of *Extension*, a Chicago magazine, regaled me with the news that my *Do You Mind If I Breathe* had their staff literally rolling on the floor. They would be sending me a check for $150.00…and did I have more.

Yes, I had at least a dozen more. And after selling to *True* and *The American Legion*, I thought I had it made. I thought wrong.

I would spend another twenty years as Director Of Communications for the Realsilk Hosiery Mills before *The Saturday Evening Post* asked to reprint one of my free-lance efforts. That beloved magazine has to date printed 154 of my original efforts.

I was recently interviewed by a sophomore high school student who asked what advice I would give to would-be writers. I believe I said it all in only these three words: "Don't give up."

Therefore, I have given up my daily grind of bikini spotter on Panama City Beach (Florida, of course) for the purpose of selecting another 30 gems from the 158 I have rendered for *The Saturday Evening Post*. The title: *Playing Leapfrog with Porcupines*.

If you like what you read, I ask only that you tell your friends, your neighbors, and your relatives—even those you don't particularly care for. If you don't agree with my outlook on marital predicaments, I would appreciate it if you kept it to yourself. Perhaps I can repay you sometime. During bikini season, that is.

Printed in the United States
5127